'*Disengagement from Education* is a valuable and
our knowledge of educational disengagement, its
remediation. This is a work which is thankfully sen
harvesting insights from a variety of different natic ___ _____
settings. *Disengagement from Education* will be well-received by
educators, researchers, policy-makers and administrators for its clarity,
coverage, organization and its commitment to effective intervention to
reduce the experience of educational failure and disconnection which
affects learners at many different levels of education.'

Richard Teese, Emeritus Professor of Education, University of Melbourne

'This invaluable and accessible book provides an outstanding review of the
issues relating to young people's disengagement from education in the UK
and internationally. It includes a thoughtful reflection on what it means to
be disengaged, an in-depth consideration of the specific challenges faced
in a range of different contexts, as well as reviews of the specific issues
relating to special educational needs, transitions, the curriculum and
pedagogy. The final chapter sets out an agenda for change. In addition,
there are many practical examples of initiatives which have been successful
in overcoming disengagement. It is written with passion and an evident
care for the disengaged and is essential reading for all of those interested
in the field whether their focus is practice or research.'

Susan Hallam, Professor of Education, UCL Institute of Education

'The impressive scope of this book shows that preventing disengagement
from education requires a holistic approach that is not a "one size fits
all" strategy. The strong focus on system responses and not simply on
the individual makes this book of real relevance for educators and
policy makers, as well as for students across professions engaging with
marginalized groups.'

Dr Paul Downes, Director, Educational Disadvantage Centre, Dublin City University

Disengagement from Education

IOEPress

Disengagement from Education

Lynne Rogers

A Trentham Book
Institute of Education Press

First published in 2015 by the Institute of Education Press, University College London, 20 Bedford Way, London WC1H 0AL

ioepress.co.uk

British Library Cataloguing in Publication Data:
A catalogue record for this publication is available from the British Library

ISBNs
978-1-85856-681-8 (paperback)
978-1-85856-682-5 (PDF eBook)
978-1-85856-683-2 (ePub eBook)
978-1-85856-684-9 (Kindle eBook)

Every effort has been made to trace copyright holders and to obtain their permission for the use of copyright material. The publisher apologizes for any errors or omissions and would be grateful if notified of any corrections that should be incorporated in future reprints or editions of this book.

The opinions expressed in this publication are those of the author and do not necessarily reflect the views of the UCL Institute of Education, University College London.

Typeset by Quadrant Infotech (India) Pvt Ltd
Printed by CPI Group (UK) Ltd, Croydon, CR0 4YY

Contents

About the author

Dr Lynne Rogers is Reader in Education at the UCL Institute of Education. She is Co-Director of the Centre for Post-14 Research and Innovation and was a founder member of the Centre for Education in the Criminal Justice System. She has long-standing interests in teacher/lecturer training and learning in further and higher education and other professional settings. During 2008–10 she was the Director of the London Centre for Excellence in Teacher Training. She has extensive experience of education as a teacher and in a range of management positions prior to becoming an academic and has undertaken research in relation to behaviour in school, disengagement from education (including the role of alternative curricula), learning, studying and homework in adolescents and issues relating to music education. She is the author of publications on behaviour and attendance in school, alternative curriculum, prison education, music education, teacher education and studying.

Preface

Education has the power to transform lives. Increasingly young people need to complete upper secondary education if they are to succeed in future employment opportunities and training and future life chances. The use of international educational comparisons and league tables means that governments internationally are working to raise attainment levels and, as a consequence, are looking at the performance and structure of education. While many developing countries struggle to provide primary and lower secondary education for all, in the developed world the issue is not access, but rather keeping young people engaged with education. Governments internationally are concerned about young people who are disengaged from education and those who drop out of education, training and employment, particularly given the central role of education in promoting economic prosperity and the social and personal welfare of individuals.

This book considers governments' attempts to address issues of disengagement from education and why, despite attempts to improve levels of engagement, disengagement remains a continuing concern. It draws together current thinking and research in the fields of education and the social sciences relating to disengagement in education among young people from age 11 to 19. The aim of the book is to focus on initiatives supporting work that seeks to engage and re-engage young people in education and to debate issues around disengagement critically. Attention is paid to issues and theories surrounding disengagement within the secondary phase of education and the strategies and interventions that are being employed throughout the world to keep young people from becoming disengaged from learning.

In contrast to other publications, a holistic approach is adopted for considering disengagement. Research indicates that disengagement describes different points or stages along a continuum and that young people move between different stages of disengagement. Existing publications often ignore the fluidity of disengagement and the notion that disengagement is a dynamic construct. Similarly, publications often focus solely on young people who could be regarded as at the extreme end of disengagement, having dropped out of education altogether, rather than explicitly acknowledging that disengagement is a process.

In line with the holistic approach, the scope of the book is deliberately ambitious, since disengagement from education crosses different educational contexts for young people aged between 11 and 19 years old. The consideration of different educational contexts gives rise to wider issues and themes that influence levels of disengagement and re-engagement with education. These include the challenges young people face during the transition between different educational settings, the barriers young people with special educational needs (SEN) may face and how alternative educational provision can enable young people to re-engage with education. These issues are further developed in chapters that focus on curriculum and pedagogy, and teaching and teacher training.

Throughout the book there are many illustrations of interventions and initiatives to support young people who are disengaged from education. Several of these are drawn from international contexts and many are based on research I have undertaken with colleagues. This includes work for the UK government, e.g. the evaluation of the Behaviour Improvement Programme and the School Exclusion Trial and research undertaken for charitable organizations, including evaluations of alternative education programmes for SkillForce and educational provision for under-25s in the criminal justice system in London for the Sir John Cass Foundation. Work that I have undertaken on initial teacher education and the experiences of prison educators is also included.

The aim of the book is to provide an evidence-based review of disengagement from education among young people aged 11 to 19. The first section sets out the context of student disengagement from education and provides definitions of disengagement, indicators of disengagement and the long-term consequences of disengagement from education. This is followed by consideration of the risk factors and precursors of disengagement, drawing on studies undertaken in the UK and internationally. The second section outlines disengagement in different educational contexts, with chapters devoted to secondary school, further education, young offender institutions and those young people regarded as not in education, employment, or training (NEET). In the third section, issues common across educational settings are explored including SEN, transitions, alternative curricula, curricula and pedagogy, and teachers and teacher training. The final section sets out how all those involved with the education and training of 11- to 19-year-olds in the developed world can best challenge disengagement from education and help break cycles of intergenerational disadvantage.

Part One

The context

1

Chapter 1

Background

This chapter sets out the issues relating to student disengagement from education: the definitions of disengagement, indicators of disengagement and the long-term consequences of disengagement from education. It considers why disengagement is of concern within many developed countries and provides an overview of policy initiatives to address disengagement.

Introduction

Disengagement from education is a complex, multi-dimensional process that falls along a continuum beginning with students who may attend lessons but appear disinterested or truant on occasional days, to the more extreme end where young people have dropped out of education entirely. In addition, many young people who remain in education may be at risk of dropping out. Disengagement from education is a more dynamic and fluid process than that implied by statistical measurement, since young people may move in and out of education and training while travelling, waiting for a college course or a job opportunity. The measurement of dropout for international comparison is only a partial indicator of disengagement from education, since no attempt is made to include young people who are at risk of disengagement. Most young people who become a statistic in terms of dropout or early school leaving have gradually become disengaged from compulsory education or training.

Throughout the world, governments, policymakers and educators have acknowledged the importance of education for promoting economic development and the social and personal welfare of individuals. Future life opportunities are influenced by participation in education and training. Children and young people who fail to complete their school education tend to be significantly disadvantaged in later life. Research suggests that they have an increased likelihood of experiencing unemployment, poorer health outcomes, worse accommodation and social status, greater risk of offending behaviour, greater susceptibility to the influences of drugs and alcohol, homelessness and anti-social behaviour, and lowered lifelong income. Young people who are disengaged from education are of concern to governments worldwide, given the associated social and economic costs in terms of increased demands for welfare support and government subsidized services. Across many countries there has been significant investment in interventions to enable young people who might be regarded as being at risk of becoming disengaged to remain in education.

The importance of secondary education

Secondary education at an international level is generally broken down into lower and upper secondary education. Lower secondary education completes the provision of basic education and builds on primary education, but in a more subject-oriented way with specialist teachers. It usually lasts for three years. Upper secondary education is seen as consolidating students' basic skills and knowledge: there is an increase in subject specialist knowledge. Students usually enter upper secondary education at the age of 15 or 16.

The distinction between lower and upper secondary education is relevant since graduating from upper secondary education is considered to be the minimum credential for successful entry into the labour market. The completion of upper secondary education has therefore become important internationally, given the increase in more knowledge-based skills needed for the labour market and the fact that workers are required to adapt to a rapidly changing global economy. Young people who leave education without upper secondary qualifications face difficulties entering and remaining in the labour force, lower wages, greater risk of poverty and greater chances of becoming an economic and social burden to society (Lyche, 2010). With reference to the challenges faced with early school leaving (ESL), the European commission commented: 'ESL represents a waste of individual life opportunities and a waste of social and economic potential' (European Commission 2010a: 4).

Over past decades, most OECD countries have seen significant increases in the educational attainment of their populations. However, this masks the increase in the number of young people regarded as NEET across many countries. Upper secondary education graduation rates differ between countries due to the variety of systems and programmes available.

Defining disengagement from education

Countries use various terms to indicate disengagement from education. At the extreme end of disengagement there is the term NEET, which originated in the UK. Canada and the US mostly use the term 'dropout', while other countries, particularly in Europe, refer to ESL. Also evident is the use of the descriptor 'at risk' to describe young people who are showing signs of disengaging or dropping out of education.

As a starting point it is helpful to consider notions of engagement, since engagement has been used as a construct to capture the process by which young people detach from school. It also helps focus attention on factors that can be altered to increase school completion rates (Appleton *et al.*, 2008). Gibbs and Foskett (2010) propose that engagement involves connectedness or a sense of belonging to school, a sense of agency, involvement, effort, commitment and concentration, motivation and interest in learning, a sense of self-efficacy, an orientation towards achievement and performance, and self-regulatory processes and skills. These features, according to Gibbs and Foskett, are outcomes or processes that contribute to engagement. By this they mean that their presence stimulates further engagement in learning in a self-perpetuating cycle of engagement. The idea of engagement as a process is important, since it tends to the notion that disengagement is also a process whereby the presence of different features may contribute to different levels of disengagement.

Researchers have conceptualized school engagement as a multidimensional construct often encompassing two or three components. The two-component model comprised emotional and behavioural dimensions (Skinner *et al.*, 2008), whereas the three-part model added cognitive engagement as the third dimension (Fredricks *et al.*, 2004). Consideration has also been given to the relationship between disengagement and behavioural indicators such as truancy and exclusion, and between grades and attainment (Balfanz *et al.*, 2007; Mac Iver and Mac Iver, 2009), as well as to the importance of student–teacher relationships and how these may impact on motivation (Montalvo *et al.*, 2007).

The problem with some definitions of young people disengaged from education, especially young people described as NEET, is that they often present disengaged young people as a homogenous group, that there is a tendency to view these categories as fixed, and that descriptions often pathologize young people.

Ross (2009: 1), based on a study of 14- to 16-year-olds in the UK, identified four different groups of disengaged or engaged young people:

- Engaged young people, who were highly engaged with school and wished to continue into higher education;
- Young people disengaged from school but not education, who disliked school and were more likely to skip classes but aspired to continue with full-time education to degree level;

- Young people who were engaged with school and wished to continue their education but not higher education;
- Disengaged young people who had lower aspirations, disliked school, and were more likely to truant.

The contribution from Ross is helpful since it draws attention to the fact that young people may be disengaged from school but not from education. However, it doesn't completely capture the fact that disengagement is not static, since students move between different levels of engagement (Callanan *et al.*, 2009). Young people vary their approaches to studying dependent on the task and their level of interest and motivation. Subject preferences, for instance, can be dependent on the relationship with the teacher. Also influential is the approach taken to teaching and learning, the flexibility and level of choice in the curriculum offer and the classroom ethos.

Disengagement from education in schools or colleges is not 'all or nothing' (Butler *et al.*, 2005). It is a process rather than a single event. In the US, while the most obvious symptom of disengagement is dropout, this is usually preceded by unsuccessful school experiences and poor attendance (Rumberger, 2011). Disengagement from education lies along a spectrum. Some young people may appear disinterested in school and the education it offers yet they continue to attend, though putting less effort into their studies. Some young people may appear disengaged in school and college, but be engaged with education outside this environment. At the extreme end are young people labelled NEET who have dropped out of education altogether. Others may have been excluded or suspended from school because their behaviour is perceived to be problematic, perhaps because they are bored, or their needs are not being met. Still others may truant or display poor attendance patterns.

While there is no universally agreed definition of disengagement, there seems to be a consensus that definitions must adopt a holistic approach that acknowledges disengagement as a complex multidimensional concept (Ross, 2009) and that definitions of disengagement need to accommodate a variety of perspectives. This approach is captured in the definition arising from the work of Baird and colleagues:

> 'Disengaged' includes those excluded permanently from school, those who have left school at leaving age, those still in school who cause disruption, experience a sense of failure or feel that the curriculum is pointless as well as those who despite succeeding in school lack interest in deep learning. Thus, disengagement would

refer to lack of involvement in academic, social or extracurricular activity or poor conduct in these contexts.

(Baird *et al.*, 2011: 140)

Labelling a young person as disengaged from education does not mean that he/she has low ambitions. In several studies where students have talked about levels of disengagement, they also spoke about wanting to achieve good grades, skills and careers. Overall students held positive aspirations and spoke about wanting to progress to further and higher education or pursue particular career pathways (Duffy and Elwood, 2013; Lloyd-Jones *et al.*, 2010).

Disengagement and participation in education

By signing the Salamanca declaration (UNESCO, 1994), countries committed themselves to the universal education of primary-age children. Since that time, many countries have extended this commitment to education for all lower secondary children. Globally, 83 per cent of lower secondary children are in either primary or secondary school, dropping to 70 per cent in low-income countries. Challenges to participation are greatest in sub-Saharan Africa and South Asia. In the majority of countries in sub-Saharan Africa, less than half of secondary-age adolescents are enrolled in school (UNICEF, 2014).

OECD data from 2012 indicates that enrolment rates among 15- to 19-year-olds, i.e. those typically in upper secondary programmes or in transition to upper levels of education, reached at least 80 per cent in 29 of the 42 OECD and partner countries with available data. High enrolment rates, 90 per cent or higher, were found in Belgium, the Czech Republic, Germany, Hungary, Ireland, Latvia, the Netherlands, Poland and Slovenia. By contrast, the proportion of young people in this age group not enrolled in education exceeded 20 per cent in Argentina, Austria, Brazil, Chile, Indonesia, Luxembourg, South Africa and the UK. In Mexico and Turkey, this proportion exceeded 40 per cent. In Colombia and China the proportion reached 57 and 66 per cent respectively (OECD, 2014a). While the focus of this book is on disengagement from education, it is important to acknowledge than in many countries young people aged 11 to 19 still have no access to education.

Estimates of the proportion of young people disengaged from education vary across different countries in relation to definitions of disengagement and how it is measured. Over a decade ago, Steedman and Stoney (2004) estimated that between a fifth and a third of all young people aged 14–16 were disengaged from education in the UK. In New Zealand, Wylie and Hipkins (2006) indicated that a third of the 14-year-old participants did not find school engaging. A fifth wanted to leave school as soon as they could.

In OECD countries, on average 20 per cent of young people drop out before finalizing upper secondary education. While some may re-engage with education later in life, one in five young people have not completed upper secondary education or the equivalent by the age of 34 (OECD, 2012a). In Australia, the proportion of teenagers disengaged from work or education has remained at around 16 per cent; this equates to 246,000 teenagers. Within this group most left school before completing Year 12 or attaining a comparable qualification (Robinson *et al.*, 2010). Within the US, the high school graduation rate is near 75 per cent (Stillwell, 2010). Graduation rates are lower amongst Hispanic and African American students compared to Asian and white students (Stillwell, 2010). While graduation rates have risen in the US, based on the available data it is estimated that one million students each year will not graduate (Richmond, 2013).

Although these comparative figures are helpful, levels of disengagement also vary within countries, by region, state or territory, and by geographical location. In the US, graduation rates range from 51.3 per cent in Nevada to 89.6 per cent in Wisconsin (Stillwell, 2010). In disadvantaged schools disengagement happens earlier (Butler *et al.*, 2005). This is a particular concern since young people in disadvantaged schools do not always have the best or most experienced teachers. In Australia, poorer students tend to be clustered in schools with poor educational outcomes that are located in economically depressed areas (Keating and Lamb, 2004).

Indicators of disengagement

Many attempts have been made to provide measurements of disengagement for two reasons. First, it can help educators identify young people at risk of disengagement before they drop out. Second, by understanding indicators of disengagement, more effective and appropriately targeted interventions can be put in place to prevent further disengagement and enable young people to re-engage with their learning.

What is problematic, though, is that disengagement is not easily defined; neither is it as measurable as other educational outcomes, such as attainment, since symptoms of engagement can be both passive and active (Sodha and Guglielmi, 2009). Disengagement is not simply a behavioural response to education: it is about the complex interaction between the young person's background and prior experiences with the ecology and geography of the educational institution (Lawson and Lawson, 2013). With these caveats in mind, researchers have used a range of indicators in an attempt to identify disengagement. In the US, attention focuses on the ABCs of disengagement: absenteeism, behaviour and course completion. Levels of high absenteeism, behaviour problems, and the failure to complete assignments and pass courses are the strongest predictors of dropping out (Mac Iver and Mac Iver, 2009). In the UK, most local authorities also use hard indicators, usually drawing on information that is held within electronic school management systems (Filmer-Sankey and McCrone, 2012).

Underachievement

Underachievement as an indicator of disengagement is based on the premise that young people who are disengaged from education achieve less well, which in turn increases the likelihood of dropping out of school. Low grades are a sign of lower preparation to progress through the educational system (Lyche, 2010). Linked to underachievement is the practice of grade repetition, where the policy in some countries is to hold young people back a year and require them to repeat that grade due to poor performance. In France, Luxembourg, Spain, Portugal and Belgium grade repetition is high and impacts on over 30 per cent of students, despite evidence that grade repetition contributes to disengagement (OECD, 2014a).

Absence

Many young people miss days from school or college because of illness, medical appointments, or due to their responsibilities as young carers. Some young people may be termed school-refusers and suffer from school phobia. While the occasional day missed from education for a genuine reason may have little impact, high levels of non-attendance are seen as an indicator of disengaging from school. Non-attenders often progressively worsen along this spectrum within each school year. Non-attendance emerges most during school transition stages such as the move from primary and secondary school (Pellegrini, 2007). There are indications that non-attendance is heterogeneous and common across gender, race and socio-economic status (Pellegrini, 2007). In most countries there is very little difference in the incidence of truancy between advantaged and disadvantaged students (OECD, 2014b). By contrast, Attwood and Croll (2006) identified low socio-economic status as a risk factor for some non-attenders.

The prevalence of young people skipping school is seen internationally. Among young people who took part in PISA 2012, 18 per cent skipped at least one class and 15 per cent skipped at least an entire day of school without authorization in the two-week period before the tests. In Argentina,

Italy, Jordan and Turkey, 40 per cent or more of students skipped at least one day of school. In the UK, almost a fifth of all teenagers admitted to skipping at least a day of lessons over this two-week period compared with less than one in a hundred in some parts of China (OECD, 2014b).

Poor attendance is a contributory factor to disengagement. High levels of non-attendance impact on achievement, which in turn impacts on the likelihood of dropping out of education. Across OECD countries, skipping days of school was associated with a 52-point lower score in maths (OECD, 2014b). Of the young people in England who miss more than 50 per cent of school, only 3 per cent achieve five or more General Certificate of Secondary Education (GCSEs) at grades A* to C, including Maths and English. Where young people have over 95 per cent attendance, 73 per cent achieve five or more GCSEs at grades A* to C (Taylor, 2012a).

Behaviour and exclusion

Across OECD countries, 70 per cent of upper secondary teachers report having students with behavioural problems in their class (OECD, 2014a). While this figure might appear alarming, most cited behaviour problems as minor, such as talking out of turn, hindering other students or causing distraction to other students (Hallam and Rogers, 2008; Sullivan *et al.*, 2014). There is no suggestion that all students disengaged with education exhibit behavioural difficulties. However, young people disengaged from education often demonstrate their frustration with the educational system by poor behaviour.

The ultimate sanction for poor behaviour is exclusion or suspension and it is this that provides another indicator of disengagement. Within England a small proportion of young people become permanently excluded from school in secondary schools. In 2012–13, 3,900 young people were permanently excluded, equivalent to 0.12 per cent of student enrolments (DfE, 2014a). Fixed-term exclusions were given to 146,070 students in 2012–13. In the US, over three million young people were suspended from school in 2010 (Losen and Gillespie, 2012). In both countries the most common reason for exclusion or suspension is disruptive behaviour.

Some groups of young people are more likely to be excluded than others. In England, boys are around three times more likely to be excluded than girls; pupils with SEN statements are around six times more likely to be excluded than those with no SEN; pupils eligible for free school meals are nearly four times more likely to be excluded than those not eligible, and young people from some ethnic groups are more likely to be excluded, including those of black Caribbean, black and white Caribbean, travellers of

Irish heritage and Gypsy/Roma heritage (DfE, 2014a). Similar inequalities are found in the US. African American students and young people with disabilities are at a far greater risk than other groups. For instance, 1 out of every 6 enrolled black students was suspended, compared with 1 in 20 white students (Losen and Gillespie, 2012).

Those who are excluded from school have poorer future outcomes than other young people. Being excluded from school is linked to an increased likelihood of having to repeat a grade, dropping out and becoming NEET, and involvement with the juvenile justice system, even after controlling for ethnicity, poverty, and school characteristics (Fabelo *et al.*, 2011).

While attainment, attendance and behaviour are not the only manifestations of disengagement, what is apparent is the interrelationship between all three.

Consequences of disengagement

Where disengaged young people are re-engaged with education, the longer-term consequences are limited. Even when young people have had short periods of being NEET, evidence suggests that many return to education or training later on (MBIE, 2013a). The real challenges arise where young people do not complete school and have low-level qualifications or have long and repeated periods as NEET.

Young people who fail to complete school tend to be significantly more disadvantaged in later life. They tend to have low levels of literacy and numeracy, which in turn can lead to low confidence and low self-esteem. They have an increased likelihood of experiencing unemployment and are at greater risk of poverty and lowered lifelong income. In addition, these young people may experience homelessness and are at greater risk of offending behaviour. They are also more susceptible to the influences of drug and alcohol misuse and antisocial behaviour (KPMG, 2009; Lyche, 2010; Nechvoglod and Beddie, 2010). Further to the long-term consequences of disengagement from education for the individual, the chance of intergenerational persistence of poverty is increased.

Policy responses to disengagement

Raising the participation age

Government reforms internationally have centred on raising the participation age in an attempt to engage young people in education for longer. Underpinning this is the belief that if young people remain in education and training, this is more likely to improve the quality of their lives, maintain a highly skilled workforce, enable the country to compete at an international level in demonstrating higher educational participation rates, and be able to respond to and compete in a changing global economy (DCSF, 2009). Indeed, it has been argued that the most significant influence on raising the participation age has been the global context (Woodin *et al.*, 2013).

The *Compact with Young Australians* (Australian Government, 2009) emphasized the need for all young people to complete Year 10 and then remain in education, employment, or training until age 17. In the UK, the 2008 Education and Skills Act raised the participation age in education and training to 17 in 2013 and 18 in 2015 (HM Government, 2008). In the US, President Barack Obama stated in his 2012 *State of the Union* address:

> When students don't walk away from their education, more of them walk the stage to get their diploma. When students are not allowed to drop out, they do better ... I am proposing that every state – every state – requires that all students stay in high school until they graduate or turn 18.
>
> (Obama, 2012)

While raising the school participation age may offer one way forward in engaging young people, it is unlikely to succeed if the education and training offered is not motivating or of interest (see Chapters 4, 6, 9 and 10).

Financial incentives

Many countries have set targets for the reduction of young people labelled as NEET. As part of their NEET-reduction strategy, some countries have implemented labour market policies that include financial incentives for employers to assist young people in making the transition to the labour market (see Chapter 6). Other financial support mechanisms include payment to young people to attend programmes of study, and allowances and scholarships to support attendance at school or college. In some countries such as the Netherlands, schools are targeted with financial incentives to reduce the number of school dropouts (Eurofound, 2012).

Interventions to prevent disengagement

Many countries have framed educational policies around the early identification of young people at risk of disengagement, so that interventions can be put in place as early as possible to support these young people before levels of disengagement become entrenched. In many instances this has been supported by the development of early warning and tracking systems to monitor levels of disengagement better. Strategies to support young people include mentoring, counselling and the use of in-school support centres (see Chapters 3 and 7).

Polices have focused on broadening the curriculum offer in schools to include more vocational provision, since there is evidence that young people disengaged from education respond better to more practical activities where they can see the relationship with the world of work (see Chapters 4 and 10). Governments have also sought to increase the flexibility of educational pathways offered to young people and, in line with this, have made efforts to improve the careers guidance given to young people who are at risk of disengaging from school (see Chapter 8).

Re-engagement
As evidenced in some countries, the development of traineeships or pre-apprenticeships provides a bridge to full apprenticeship programmes of study (see Chapter 4). Most countries have sought to further develop and raise the standard of their alternative educational provision for those who struggle in mainstream settings in an attempt to re-engage young people in learning and to set them on more positive future pathways (see Chapters 7 and 9). In other countries, such as Australia, there has been an increase in school-based vocational provision. This in an attempt to offer a more engaging and relevant curriculum.

Reintegration
Where young people have disengaged from education completely, second-chance opportunities have been put in place to reintegrate them into education and training (see Chapter 6). Often this requires intensive one-to-one support and counselling. For young people in the criminal justice system the reintegration into the community is especially important, since education is one way to reduce re-offending (see Chapter 5).

The quality of teaching and learning
Government-led initiatives worldwide have focused on raising the standard and quality of teaching that young people experience. Among young people disengaged from education, this has included the promotion of a more inclusive approach to education where the experiences and interests of all are valued. Allied to this has been the promotion of pedagogic approaches that engage and motivate young people (see Chapters 10 and 11).

Endnote
There is no agreed definition of disengaged students. Current definitions often overlap due to the complexity of disengagement. Disengagement lies along a continuum. Nearly all young people will be disengaged from education at some point. Similarly, many young people experience being NEET for short periods in their life. What matters is the extent or level of disengagement

and its duration. Where young people are disengaged from education for long periods of time, the long-term consequences are profoundly negative in relation to employment, life chances, health and well-being. In addition, long-term disengagement can lead to intergenerational poverty.

Disengagement from education does not necessarily mean that young people are not interested in education: rather, it may indicate that young people are not interested in the educational offer in schools or colleges.

Policy responses tend to focus on measures to prevent disengagement, to re-engage young people with education, and to reintegrate young people into education and training. Too often they seem to present disengagement as a crisis without acknowledging the continuum of need and support that young people at different stages of disengagement may require. In turn, coverage in the press often tends to pathologize young people who are disengaged from education.

Chapter summary

- Government concern with disengagement among young people centres on the role education plays in promoting economic development and the social and personal welfare of individuals.
- Increasingly, young people require upper secondary qualifications if they are to gain employment.
- Disengagement from education is a multi-dimensional concept involving many factors that sit along a continuum.
- Attempts to identify young people at risk of disengagement usually focus on the use of hard indicators such as attainment, attendance and absence.
- Long-term consequences of high levels of disengagement are: poor employment prospects, lower earning levels, poor health and well-being.
- Policies to reduce disengagement include raising the participation age, financial incentives, more flexible curricula, alternative educational provision and second-chance opportunities.

Chapter 2

Understanding disengagement

This chapter outlines research relating to the risk factors and precursors of disengagement, drawing on studies undertaken in the UK and internationally. Attention is given to factors operating at the level of the family and the individual, within educational institutions, and relating to demographic characteristics. The cumulative impact of risk factors and the contribution made by protective factors are considered.

Context

Any attempt to explain what underpins educational disengagement is challenging. While evidence suggests that many young people disengaged from education exhibit poor attendance, poor academic attainment and poor behaviour, it is difficult to ascertain the triggers for disengagement given the circularity of cause and effect (Lloyd-Jones *et al.*, 2010). Poor attendance, for instance, often presents young people with the additional challenge of catching up on missed work and yet all too often too few opportunities are presented for this. The accumulative effect of missing work and being unable to catch up can lead to disengagement from school. Similarly, it is not straightforward to differentiate between factors that cause or lead to being NEET and factors that only correlate with being NEET (Farrington and Welsh, 2003; 2007). Furthermore, young people disengage from education for different reasons.

Multiple factors are associated with increasing the risk of young people becoming disengaged from education. These include factors at the level of the individual, the family, and the educational institution or context, in addition to demographic factors and economic settings. It is the cumulative mix of and the interaction between these factors that contribute to disengagement. What is clear is that risk factors do not impact in a similar manner on the educational engagement of all young people. For instance, many young people experiencing high levels of poverty and disadvantage succeed in and remain engaged with education despite the challenges that they face. In part it is the complexity of risk factors leading to disengagement that presents the challenge to educators, since no factor alone accounts for disengagement or dropout.

While some factors may be viewed as fixed, for example parental education level, many factors are amenable to change, such as the systems and processes of education that are in operation in different educational environments. Educational institutions, be they schools, colleges or young offender institutions (YOIs) have an important role to play in preventing young people from becoming disengaged with education and in fostering re-engagement. As Dale (2010) comments, all too often the school composition can propel young people towards disengagement rather than inhibiting that trajectory.

Perspectives on disengagement

In the UK, Ofsted (2010a: 7–8) described young people who had not completed school and were NEET as having low levels of literacy and numeracy, poor school attendance and unsatisfactory behaviour that led them to, or put them at risk of, exclusion. The young people included those with a learning difficulty and/or disability; teenage mothers and pregnant teenagers; young carers; those with health problems, including mental health issues; young people from disadvantaged or challenging family backgrounds; those with complex social and emotional needs; young people at risk of offending and those leaving a custodial establishment; young people who were gifted and talented but had become bored with school; those from low-income families where there was a tradition of adults not being in employment, training or further or higher education; and some young people from certain minority ethnic backgrounds. Implicit in this description are a number of factors which placed the young people as risk of being NEET, for example family background, prior attainment, health and well-being.

While this description draws on the perspective of Ofsted inspectors, who are part of a regulatory inspection body in the UK, other research enables the voices of young people themselves to be heard. As part of a larger study, Callanan and Morrell (2013) interviewed 16- to 18-year-olds currently, previously, or at risk of becoming NEET. The participants gave various reasons for dropping out of education. Some young people reported preferring to leave school at age 16 due to negative school experiences that included bullying, poor relationships with teachers and peers, and disengagement from the school curriculum. Taken together, these experiences deterred them from remaining in education and influenced their decision to look for employment. Some of the young people also felt that gaining work experience and embarking on the career ladder earlier would be beneficial, which echoes other research findings in that young people disengaged from education do have career ambitions and aspirations (Duffy and Elwood, 2013; Lloyd-Jones *et al.*, 2010). Participants in the study by Callanan and Morrell (2013) did, though, experience multiple barriers to employment including their low level of qualifications.

These young people also outlined several barriers to accessing and sustaining education. Barriers included poor school experiences, leading to low attainment at age 16, which in turn limited the options for further study available to them. Reasons for dropping out of post-compulsory education included struggling to keep up academically, lack of support for SEN, homelessness and family crises, and financial barriers. The young people often described multiple aborted attempts to find and sustain education and training opportunities (Callanan and Morrell, 2013).

Risk factors and disengagement

There is no universally agreed definition of disengagement. Researchers have approached disengagement from different disciplines, such as psychology and sociology, and have developed different models of disengagement. Ideas stemming from psychology have often focused on the place that motivation, attitudes, and thinking play in fostering engagement, in contrast to sociological perspectives, which have tended to concentrate on well-being and belonging. Research into disengagement also takes different methodological perspectives. Some centres on qualitative studies to understand and explore young people's perceptions of the process of disengagement, for example, whereas other research analyses quantitative data, often of a longitudinal nature, using multivariate statistical techniques to predict factors associated with disengagement. Yet other research looks at interventions to combat disengagement in comparison with control groups, so as to evaluate what works best.

Given the diversity in approaches to exploring disengagement, researchers have put forward different factors and variables that are thought to contribute to disengagement. Rumberger and Lin (2009) in the US identified two broad factors. The first focused on factors associated with the individual characteristics of students and the second on factors associated with the institutional characteristics of their families, schools and communities. Individual characteristics referred to the educational performance, behaviours, attitudes and backgrounds of the young people. Callanan *et al.* (2009) in the UK described causes of disengagement in terms of factors within or external to the school system. In addition, the influence of peer groups, aspirations, and future plans were seen as cross-over factors. This was similar to the approach taken by KPMG in Australia (2009). Sodha and Guglielmi (2009), also in the UK, outlined three overarching factors contributing to disengagement: child-level risk factors, environmental-level risk factors and structural factors. In a report for the European Commission, Dale (2010) identified five levels that increased the risk of early school leaving: family and community, schooling, pupil and peers, the education system, and employment and training. To give an indication of the breadth of factors associated with disengagement from education, the five levels identified by Dale contained 43 major factors with 190 subcategories.

Some researchers have placed an emphasis on the distinction between fixed and alterable factors. Fixed factors refer to those that are too difficult or impracticable to address, such as parental educational level and socio-economic status. Much of the work in this area has drawn on Finn's (1989) developmental model of school dropout, labelled the participation-identification model. This model implies that all those working with disengaged young people should focus interventions on factors where change is possible. An example is the Check and Connect programme in the US, where these principles have been applied in the structuring of this state-wide mentoring programme (Christenson and Reschly, 2010).

While there are differences in the approaches taken to researching disengagement from education, in broad terms there is an appreciation that family factors including socio-economic status, family structure and parental education; demographic factors including gender, ethnicity and location; individual factors such as aspirations, prior achievement, past experiences and SEN; and the educational context including the curricula, grade repetition or retention, and student–teacher relationships; are important (see for example Rumberger and Lim, 2009, in the US; KPMG, 2009, in Australia; Dale, 2010, in Europe). In addition, economic settings and labour market conditions shape and influence decisions regarding leaving school early (Cedefop, 2010; Dale, 2010).

Before I review the factors that contribute to young people's vulnerability towards disengagement, two caveats need to be mentioned. First, research can only indicate associations between factors and an increased risk of disengagement; this is not the same as causality. Second, the discussion presented here focuses on the main findings arising from research. Regardless of which factor is considered, there is often some evidence that suggests that the factor may have less influence than is widely perceived. As an example, Homel *et al.* (2012), in their multivariate analysis of Longitudinal Surveys of Australian Youth and Youth in Focus study data, suggested that parental education levels were less influential in decisions to leave school early than poor school experiences, participation in risky activities and educational aspirations.

This contrasts with research that indicates that parental educational levels are strongly related to disengagement and early school leaving.

Family factors

High levels of poverty can contribute to disengagement. Having a higher socio-economic status is associated with higher educational attainment (Cedefop, 2010; Traag and van der Velden, 2011). Parents who have higher levels of earning also tend to participate in more cultural activities, which is linked to lower levels of dropout. The level of family income influences the extent to which parents/carers can provide resources to support their children's education through after-school clubs and extra-curricular activities and to provide support for learning within the home (Rumberger, 2011).

Levels of parental education also contribute to disengagement. Young people whose parents did not complete upper secondary education are more likely to be at risk of disengagement. Lower levels of parental education are associated with poorer educational outcomes for young people and are linked to early school leaving (Dale, 2010; Robinson *et al.*, 2010; Traag and van der Velden, 2011). Some studies have indicated that the mother's highest qualification level and the quality of the home learning environment are among the strongest predictors of outcomes at ages 10 and 11 (Sodha and Guglielmi, 2009). In the Netherlands, for each additional year of parent education, the risk of a young person dropping out of school decreased by approximately 7 per cent (Traag and van der Velden, 2011). Parental education level also influences the educational achievements of young people, for instance in relation to staying in or leaving school.

Family structure, the number and types of individuals in a child's household are also influential. Young people from single parent families are more at risk of dropping out (Dale, 2010; Lyche, 2010). Where young people have parents who are homeless or unemployed, this too increases the risk of dropping out from education (Lyche, 2010).

In addition, parenting practices influence academic achievement and in turn have a bearing on disengagement. Positive parent–child relationships and interactions lead to better developmental outcomes for children and young people. Early school leavers are often from families characterized by parenting styles that include lower levels of supervision, low aspirations for children's schooling, less parental engagement with school, negative reactions to underachievement in school, less verbal interaction between mothers and children, and situations where parents are more likely to leave their offspring to make their own decisions (Dale, 2010: 19).

Individual factors

A range of risk factors can affect the young person, including low levels of language, literacy and maths, low aspirations, SEN, prior life experiences, and low levels of social, emotional and behavioural competence.

Poor levels of literacy, language and maths

Young people who have not acquired good levels of literacy and numeracy are more likely to become frustrated and disengaged with their learning. In England, one in six children leave primary school having failed to master basic reading skills (DfE, 2012a). Ordinary day-to-day teaching generally does not enable children with literacy difficulties to catch up with their peers. Many young people arrive in secondary school without the necessary literacy and numeracy skills (OECD, 2012a).

There are links between poor attainment in maths and truancy. In England, analysis of data from 2006 showed that Year 9 pupils entering secondary schools with poor maths skills were over twice as likely to truant as those who entered with age-appropriate skills (Every Child a Chance Trust, 2009a). Young people with poor numeracy skills are more likely than their peers to be excluded from school. Truancy rates are four times higher in secondary school for children who were very poor readers at the end of primary school and more than double for the children who had very low levels of numeracy (Every Child a Chance Trust, 2009a; 2009b). It is self-evident that poor literacy and numeracy skills impact on attainment.

Aspirations

Low aspirations are linked with poorer educational outcomes. Aspirations may be associated with beliefs about ability and are influenced by self-esteem (Strand and Winston, 2008). This suggests that there is a reciprocal relationship between aspirations and attainment, since aspirations may predict educational achievement but can also be an outcome of it. Groups that are particularly at risk of lower aspirations are boys, young people from some minority ethnic groups, and young people from disadvantaged backgrounds.

Using the construct of possible selves to investigate aspirations, Mainwaring and Hallam (2010) found that, compared to their peers in mainstream education, young people in Pupil Referral Units (PRUs) had fragile positive selves and more negative perceptions of their prospects. Baird *et al.* (2012) indicated that the aspirations of learners in further education (FE) tended to be lower than those of students who continued their studies in school sixth forms post-16. Young people in FE in England are more disadvantaged than their peers in school sixth forms. In the Netherlands, young people who had plans and preferences for their future, high levels of motivation, and more mature cognitive capacities were found to be more likely to stay in school or follow recommended pathways than students who did not (Traag and van der Velden, 2011).

Other research draws attention to the notion of an aspiration–achievement gap, with higher aspirations not always translating into better outcomes (Sodha and Guglielmi, 2009). Menzies (2013) suggests that although students from disadvantaged backgrounds may often have high aspirations for their education, they may not know how to achieve them and can struggle to maintain them.

Special educational needs

Young people with SEN have a higher risk of disengagement from education than those without. They are disproportionally represented among those who drop out of school and gain fewer qualifications at secondary level than their peers. This is true in many countries. In the US, students with disabilities have much higher dropout rates than other students (Rumberger and Lim, 2009). Across Europe, young people who leave school early are more likely to come from disadvantaged groups, including those who have SEN (Dale, 2010).

Fuller attention is given to young people who have SEN in Chapter 7. Some disengage because of the way in which schools deal with the issue of SEN. SEN as a label can be seen to reflect low levels of achievement as well as disengagement, even when this might be due to low teacher expectations (Steer, 2009). Often, young people have undiagnosed SEN, which impacts on their level of disengagement and may lead to poor behaviour.

Previous life experiences

For some young people previous life experiences are risk factors that contribute to disengagement from education. These might include experiencing some form of trauma or abuse, or family violence. Children who have experienced early, chronic trauma, including family or community violence, can develop emotional, behavioural, cognitive and relationship difficulties that make it hard for them to learn and function effectively in school (Cole *et al.*, 2005). While individual responses vary, exposure to trauma is associated with a higher risk of school dropout (Porche *et al.*, 2011).

Some young people are looked after or placed in out-of-home care. Looked-after children are over-represented in exclusion and truancy figures. Health issues within the family and bereavement can also contribute to disengagement, as can the experience of being a young carer. Some children have primary caring responsibilities for parents who have profound physical disabilities, are terminally ill or have psychiatric problems. The impact of caring on the child's education can be immense.

Demographic factors

Much research, though not all, indicates that dropout rates are higher for males than for females (Cedefop, 2010; Dale, 2010). Young people from certain groups are more likely to become disengaged from education. In the US, this includes black and Hispanic young people (Chapman *et al.*, 2010) and young people from Māori backgrounds in Australia (MBIE, 2013b). Often, though, differences can be explained by other factors such as family background or educational performance. In Hungary, there is a tendency to place children from disadvantaged backgrounds, particularly Roma children, in special education institutions that are often characterized by low expectations and staffed by teachers who are insufficiently trained to work in multicultural classes (Szira and Nemeth, 2007). Studies have explored immigration status as a risk factor contributing to disengagement, although this tends to be compounded by language proficiency.

Institutional factors

The culture and emotional climate of educational institutions, be they schools, colleges, YOIs, or alternative educational providers, influences student engagement, as does their approach to teaching and learning. Educational institutions where there are positive student–teacher relationships tend to have lower dropout rates (Mac Iver and Mac Iver, 2009). Ineffective behaviour policies and approaches to behaviour are also risk factors. Where there is a mismatch between the way a young person learns and the norms of the institution, young people can be left feeling disconnected from school, teachers and peers because of their poor academic performance (Dale, 2010).

The size, type and location of the educational institution are also significant. In the US, after controlling for school demographics such as ethnicity and poverty, attendance and resourcing, higher dropout rates were evident in schools that were large, located in urban settings and public (Rumberger and Thomas, 2000). In the Netherlands, schools with high ethnic diversity show higher dropout rates (Traag and van der Velden, 2011). In large schools, young people may find it harder to create positive relationships with their teachers and peers (KPMG, 2009); larger class sizes may also contribute to disengagement since they can reduce the potential for personalized learning or individual attention. Indeed, much alternative educational provision takes places in small classes that emphasize developing strong relationships between students and teachers. Schools serving disadvantaged young people often recruit less experienced and less competent teachers.

Relevant, too, is the level of flexibility within the curriculum, including alternatives to mainstream provision (see Chapters 4 and 10). Failure to provide young people with alternatives to mainstream education places them at greater risk of disengagement (Cedefop, 2010; Traag and van der Velden, 2011). Where the vocational offer is poor, then, young people are similarly at greater risk of disengagement.

In a UK study, Ross (2009) indicated that those most at risk of disengaging were white males and young people from disadvantaged backgrounds. The factors that seemed to affect engagement included schools working with parents and parental aspirations, information and guidance, homework supervision, extra-curricular activities, study support, quality of relationships with teachers, the curriculum, bullying and school levels of truancy.

Interrelationship between factors

Almost all young people experience a number of challenges or risks during their time in education and training that might lead them to becoming disengaged. For instance, most young children experience the transition from primary to secondary education. While the majority make it successfully, some are vulnerable to disengagement at this point because of risk factors such as SEN, or because they are from disadvantaged backgrounds or at risk of exclusion.

No one risk factor predicts disengagement from education. Risk factors do not operate alone, but in combination and interaction with other risk and preventative or protective factors. It is the combination of risk factors that increases the vulnerability of young people over time to becoming disengaged from education and training (KPMG, 2009). An important point is that different risk factors mediate with one another across different contexts and the interrelationship between different factors. For instance, while there is a strong correlation between educational performance and disengagement and dropout, attainment grades are influenced by social background, gender, cultural capital (Lyche, 2010), parents' education and the labour market. There are clear interactions between poverty and disadvantage and young people's experiences of education and training.

The extent to which factors affect disengagement depends on their relative strength and on potential triggers and stressors. The more risk factors, the greater the likelihood of disengagement from education.

Protective factors

Protective factors can reduce the impact of different risk factors. Offering relevant and meaningful curricula tailored to the interests, abilities and aspirations of young people can be a valuable protective factor against disengagement from education (Callanan *et al.*, 2009; KPMG, 2009). To be effective, the curriculum needs to be matched to the levels of the learners so that they have opportunities for success, which in turn enable them to develop their self-esteem and self-confidence in learning (see Chapters 5, 7 and 10). For some young people, the provision of vocational pathways or alternative education can re-engage them in learning, especially where learners are able to see the relevance of the curriculum offer to the world of work (see Chapters 4 and 9). Where young people find the traditional school environment difficult, alternative educational contexts can be a protective factor.

Clear aspirations and having a clear pathway in place are major protective factors that can mitigate against disengagement from education (Callanan *et al.*, 2009). This necessitates providing effective information, advice and guidance (IAG) and, in some cases, mentoring and counselling to support young people to develop clear aspirations and also to ensure that flexible pathways are in place to enable them to be achieved (see Chapters 3, 4 and 6). Interestingly, the young people in a study of truanting said they were less likely to truant if they had received careers advice or had opportunities to undertake work experience as part of their studies (McIntosh and Houghton, 2005).

Positive student–teacher relationships are particularly important as protective factors, as are adult role models (see Chapters 3, 4, 9 and 11). Educational practitioners can do much to foster strong supportive relationships. Where strong relationships are in place and young people feel they are treated with respect, they report working harder and attending lessons more regularly (Callanan *et al.*, 2009).

Transitions can be particularly challenging for those at risk of disengagement and for those reintegrating into mainstream education. Interventions prior to transition and continued support after transition can be a protective factor (see Chapters 5 and 8).

Positive relationships with peers, between the home and school, and within the community, are also important protective factors. Families that can provide encouragement and support for learning, including support with homework, can help protect their children from becoming disengaged from education. For young people with higher level or more complex needs, a protective factor will be access to specialist support.

Endnote

Multiple risk factors contribute to disengagement from education, to leaving school early, or to dropping out. No one risk factor predicts disengagement; rather, multiple factors are involved. It is the interaction between the factors, and their severity and combination that contribute to disengagement. Young people disengage from education for different reasons, but most describe a process of disengagement rather than a response to a particular event or crisis. It is important to note, however, that risk factors are only associated with disengagement and do not indicate causality. Not all young people disengaged from education, for instance, are poor achievers, even though low academic attainment has a strong association with disengagement. Understanding risk factors is important, since protective factors are often the converse. An understanding of risk factors affords strong indications of protective factors that are amenable to interventions. Schools and colleges can focus on these to re-engage young people and prevent them from becoming disengaged. As yet, more research is needed to understand how protective factors operate and how young people who are vulnerable to disengagement can develop notions of resilience to enable them to remain in education and training.

Chapter summary

The risk of young people becoming disengaged from education is associated with a multiplicity of factors:

- Family factors include levels of parental education, parenting styles, the family structure and socio-economic status.
- Individual factors include language, literacy and numeracy skills, SEN, aspirations and life experiences.
- Institutional factors include size and location, ethos, the learning environment, the curriculum, relationships with teachers and peers and levels of support and guidance.
- Demographic factors include gender, ethnicity and additional language proficiency for immigrant students.

Protective factors can ameliorate the impact of risk factors. All those involved in the education and training of young people at risk of becoming, or already disengaged from education need to focus on the factors that are amenable to change.

Part Two

Disengagement
across contexts

Chapter 3

Secondary school

This chapter explores issues concerning young people in mainstream secondary education: how they are identified as being at risk of disengagement, the importance of early intervention, and the continuum of support schools put in place. The focus is on school-based interventions. Case study examples are given of Learning Support Units/in-house student support centres, learning mentors, counsellors, flexible timetabling and managed moves.

Context

Internationally, increasing numbers are attending lower and upper secondary education. Many governments across the developed world have made clear commitments to improve the outcomes of young people who are at risk of disengaging from education, as evidenced by policy guidelines and initiatives in secondary schools. When we view disengagement from education as a continuum, it is clear that secondary school pupils at different points on this continuum will need different levels of support to prevent their becoming disengaged when they might be at risk of dropping out. For some pupils, school-wide reforms such as student-centred approaches to teaching and learning and a positive school ethos make a difference to their sense of belonging and feeling valued (see Chapters 10 and 11). Others, though, will need in-school interventions that focus on one-to-one support from mentors or counsellors, for instance, while young people with more complex needs may require a range of interventions including time spent in a specialist student support centre. And for a minority of young people, the best way forward will be a managed move to another school or educational setting.

This need for varied support is apparent in the tiered provision for students at risk of disengagement in countries such as Australia, Canada and the US. One example from England will suffice. At-risk children were identified in the light of criteria relating to exclusion, attendance and risk of engaging with crime. Three tiers of potential risk were identified, each requiring increasing levels of support from schools, in partnership with relevant agencies as appropriate. Named key workers supported children at each tier. Level 1 entailed targeted support within the local school from a range of relevant professionals, level 2 provided intensive support with the local school from a range of relevant professionals, and level 3 required rapid response from a range of appropriate agencies (Hallam and Rogers, 2008).

Early intervention

Early intervention is taken to mean intervening as quickly as possible when difficulties and problems first emerge, irrespective of the pupil's age. This is in line with the Policy Review of Children and Young People (HM Treasury and DfES, 2007: 12): 'Early intervention means intervening as soon as possible to tackle problems that have already emerged for children and young people', and contrasts with perspectives on early intervention that focus on early childhood experiences.

Early intervention targets specific children and young people who have an identified need for additional support once problems have begun to emerge, but before they become serious (Walker and Donaldson, 2011). Identifying young people at risk of disengagement is not without difficulties. While some may manifest disengagement by poor attendance or behaviour, others might appear withdrawn and quiet, which can be more difficult for schools to identify. Schools vary considerably in how they define at-risk young people prior to putting an intervention in place. One reason research into interventions produces poor results is that they have not targeted the pupils most in need of support (Archive Incorporated, 2006).

Various tools have been developed to assist schools in identifying young people at risk of disengagement. The Students Mapping Tool was developed and implemented in Australia in 2007 to assist schools in identifying students who have characteristics that place them at risk of early school leaving (DEECD, 2010). In the US, many states have developed early warning systems. Virginia for example uses the Virginia Early Warning System (VEWs) developed by its Department of Education. VEWs enables the identification of students at risk of dropping out based on attendance, behaviour, course completion and their level of risk (Bruce *et al.*, 2011).

Within the School Exclusion Trial (IOE and NFER, 2014), all schools recognized the importance of early intervention. As one assistant head teacher observed:

> I think all schools would acknowledge the earlier they intervene
> the greater the likelihood of success. We identify students from

our nurture groups with discussion from the primary schools and who they think has got issues, and information coming through from primary level.

(IOE and NFER, 2014: 54)

Many schools had set up central databases to record and monitor information when they started working with the young people and their families. Staff used the database to identify patterns of behaviour and barriers to learning, and to seek patterns among those vulnerable to exclusion, including pupils with SEN or on free schools meals.

Many schools constantly monitored and tracked data to ensure that the needs of the young people were met and their progression regularly reviewed. The assistant head teacher of one school spoke about weekly meetings with the head of maths and the assistant director who was responsible for monitoring. They held weekly meetings with the support and welfare team to look at behaviour. As a group, the staff brainstormed the pupils who had behaviour issues and considered the various initial interventions to make. When students made decisions about their curriculum choices at the end of Key Stage 3, a huge amount of work went into providing information and advice, to ensure that anyone showing signs of disengagement had the right package of courses (see Chapter 8 for the importance of information, advice and guidance for young people).

Types of support

In a review of programmes for 14- to 16-year-olds at risk of temporary disconnection from learning – by which the authors meant those who did not face multiple and complex barriers to engagement in education, employment or training – schools had put in place two or more approaches to prevent disengagement. These might involve mentoring schemes, employer involvement, alternative curricula or careers guidance. Most students selected for the extra support were either not achieving their potential academically or had mild behavioural issues (Kettlewell *et al.*, 2012). The authors concluded that this reflected the findings of previous research (e.g. Filmer-Sankey and McCrone, 2012) that young people at risk of temporary disconnection tend not to have complex needs.

In 2012–13, out of a list of 22 possible in-school interventions to support at-risk pupils (IOE and NFER, 2014), the number that was in place in schools ranged from 7 to 22, with a mean of 15. These included interventions to support anger management, behaviour management or support, the use of student support centres, teaching assistant support, counselling, school–home liaison, and timetable changes. During the evaluation, the use of inclusion/learning support units increased in all schools. Learning support units, inclusion coordinators and revised school timetables were considered effective in preventing exclusions, improving attendance, improving attainment and improving behaviour.

Interventions to address young people's needs in school settings in Australia include school-based mentoring programmes, tutoring programmes, referrals to specialist services or student support services and breakfast and homework clubs (DEECD, 2010). In Canada, school-based interventions include special education support, tutoring, coaching and community agency support. In Ontario, all high schools have Student Success Teams, comprising the principal, student success teacher, guidance counsellor, special education teacher, and other educators, who provide extra attention to the students who need it (Ontario Ministry of Education, 2011).

One-to-one support

Mentoring

The mentoring of students is extremely popular throughout the world. Big Brothers Big Sisters, for instance, serves more than 200,000 children in the US, has more than 200,000 volunteer mentors and has affiliates in 11 countries including Israel, Poland, Canada and New Zealand (Big Brothers Big Sisters, 2014). Mentoring programmes worldwide vary depending on whether they are based in schools or the community and also on the type of support offered, whether informally or on a weekly basis. Nearly all mentoring programmes are based on the notion of developing supportive relationships between young people and non-parental adults or older peers. It is these trust-based relationships that enable the needs of the young people to be met (Eby *et al.*, 2008). Adults might be volunteers or employed within the school setting. Mentoring programmes in the US serve thousands of children and young people each year (Wheeler *et al.*, 2010), many of whom are perceived to be at risk of academic failure, substance abuse, harmful peer relationships or other negative outcomes.

School-based mentoring programmes can have different goals. Some are concerned with school-related behaviour and academic performance, while others focus on providing support for young people during times of personal or social stress and guidance for decision making. Some mentoring provision is specifically for students who are perceived to be academically at risk, while other programmes may focus on building self-esteem. Their duration can vary, although evidence suggests that more prolonged mentoring relationships, with frequent and consistent meetings that are characterized by a strong emotional bond, are associated with better outcomes (Rhodes and DuBois, 2006).

It has also been popular to involve undergraduate students in mentoring students who are at risk. In the US, GEAR-UP, Gaining Early Awareness and Readiness for Undergraduate Program, uses college students to mentor and act as role models for low-income students. In Israel, the Students Build a Neighbourhood programme matches Ethiopian children who are academically and socially challenged with young Israeli students. The mentors help with homework and engage their mentees in sports and other extra-curricular activities, but also serve as role models.

In South Korea, one particular mentoring intervention sought to narrow the attainment gap between its affluent and low-income youths (Choi and Lemberger, 2010). It was responding to overall school performance in South Korea where, although internationally performance was good, within the country stark divisions had been created between the achievement outcomes of its affluent and low-income youths. Students were mentored by undergraduate students who received training and supervision throughout the programme. Academic outcomes were positive, with significant gains made in maths and reading (Choi and Lemberger, 2010).

In the UK, interest has focused on learning mentors operating with disengaged pupils in primary and secondary schools. Initially introduced as part of the Excellence in Cities initiative in 1999, the use of learning mentors extended through other educational programmes. Learning mentors were employed in schools as a means of raising the aspirations of and outcomes for young people, to help break down barriers to learning, improve attendance and reduce exclusion (DfES, 2005a; 2005b). A particular strength of the learning mentors' role is that they can focus on particular needs as they arise and thus tailor their approach to facilitate re-engagement with education. For an example see Box 3.1.

> **BOX 3.1 A** SHORT-TERM SINGLE LEVEL INTERVENTION WITH A
> LEARNING MENTOR
> Natalie began experiencing difficulties during Year 7 at school
> and at home. She refused to complete homework, was rude to the
> teachers and as she said, 'things were becoming difficult'. Her mother
> approached the school and Natalie was assigned to the senior learning
> mentor from the BEST [Behaviour and Education Support Team]. She
> had weekly one-to-one sessions where she was able to talk through
> problems and was given the opportunity to reflect on her behaviour
> both in and out of school. Now in Year 8, she spoke about how things
> had changed for her, how she was a 'different person', and that her
> behaviour, attitude and approach to school and home were different.
> Without the opportunity to spend time with the learning mentor,
> Natalie felt that her behaviour would have become much worse and
> that she may, ultimately, have been excluded.
>
> (Hallam and Rogers, 2008: 198)

Counselling

School-based counselling services operate in many countries. In the UK an estimated 70,000–90,000 young people access counselling in schools each year (Cooper, 2013). In the US and Canada, the term Guidance Services is often adopted to describe the goal of those who aim to support the personal, social, emotional and academic development of young people (Sink *et al.*, 2008). In Hong Kong, school-based counselling is provided by the government, non-government organizations and the private sector. As practised in the UK, school-based counselling is usually person-centred and is a relatively non-directive form of therapy (Rupani *et al.*, 2012), influenced by the work of Carl Rogers and humanistic approaches to psychology. In the US, interventions are generally group-based, and of a cognitive/behavioural or relatively directive nature (Baskin *et al.*, 2010).

For some young people, counselling brings about change in a relatively short space of time; for others the process may take longer (see Box 3.2). Throughout the School Exclusion Trial (IOE and NFER, 2014), a number of young people received counselling as part of a range of interventions to support their re-engagement. In one school the student support centre provided a base for school counsellors so that students could visit the centre and discuss problems and concerns throughout the school day.

Box 3.2 Year-long counselling support for bereavement
Lisa was in Year 8 and went through two bereavements in a short space of time. Her grandfather died and three days later her best friend since nursery died from cancer. Lisa was very depressed and very angry about the deaths and experienced moody rages. Some days she found herself crying a lot and on others she would be in a rage, not wishing to do anything at school and getting into trouble. 'I was holding everything back since none of my friends understood because they had never been through anything like this. I couldn't really talk about it with my Mum, because she also had her own stresses since it was her Dad that had died. I didn't have anyone to speak to. My Head of Year referred me to the counsellor. It has been really good. If I get upset about things, I can come here and talk about it. Things have changed a lot for me: before I was stressed out and I was quite snappy, but now I know I don't have to put a brave face on, I can talk things through rather than putting a mask on. Usually I come once a week, but I also pop in if I'm having a bad day. A bad day either means that I just cry or I just won't want to do anything and I'll be very difficult. Little things just trigger me off and I'll be in a bad mood. Or I'll remember about the deaths and I'll feel really depressed. The school has been really helpful and put everything into place for me really quickly. I'm learning now how to cope with it all. I still go through some bad days and moody rages, but I'm able to work things through. Before, my work wasn't very good and I was getting dragged into lots of trouble in and out of the classroom. I wasn't getting on with my work. Now my work has improved and the teachers are impressed. If I hadn't been able to see the counsellor I think I would have become more angry. I would probably have got into fights and I may have been excluded.'

(Hallam *et al.*, 2005: 144)

Critical to the success of one-to-one interventions by learning mentors and counsellors is the development of supportive relationships, the opportunities for young people to discuss problems, and the availability of flexible access if difficulties arise during the school day.

Specialist support centres

Learning Support Units (LSUs) are school-based centres for pupils who are disengaged, at risk of exclusion, or vulnerable because of family or social issues. Originally called in-school centres, they have reduced permanent exclusions (Hallam and Castle, 1999). LSUs have been successful in improving behaviour and attendance (Ofsted, 2006). The term LSU is a generic term for school centres or units that provide short-term teaching and support programmes that are tailored to the needs of pupils who need help in improving their behaviour, attendance, or attitude to learning. Some schools have a specific name for their centre but all aim to keep young people in school and learning, and to provide opportunities for the issues that might be concerning them to be tackled. It is intended that students be reintegrated into mainstream classes as soon as possible. Similar to alternative education provision (see Chapter 9), the number of students attending these support centres is usually small. They may have different attendance patterns such as full- or part-time, the latter spending the remaining time with their class. Often students attend the specialist provision during lessons with which they have particular difficulties.

Overwhelmingly, trial schools in the School Exclusion Trial were taking an increased moral and practical responsibility for pupils at risk of exclusion and this meant they were working to place young people in the most appropriate provision (IOE and NFER, 2014). Many schools made use of multi-agency provision to support the most vulnerable pupils.

In one school, a support centre had been established to meet the needs of a small group of pupils who presented behaviour-related issues that would have culminated in permanent exclusion. The focus was to provide in the school the educational, social and emotional interventions to maintain the pupils in education. The centre had evolved to operate around a nurture group system for the school's most vulnerable pupils, providing support through small groups, breakfast or lunch clubs.

In another local authority, one secondary school had developed a strong commitment to inclusion and pastoral support, a central element of which was a dedicated centre for pupil support. The centre supported the individual needs of all students through the creation of bespoke packages of provision, interventions, alternative curricula and pathways, generally delivered in-house and on-site with very little external provision commissioned. Key to the approach was that the school looked to itself and its partners and stakeholders, including the wider parent/carer community, to find opportunities for supporting all its pupils, not just those identified as being at risk of exclusion. Critical within this whole school approach was the way the centre strategically identified pupils at the youngest possible age, unlike the traditional crisis intervention or provision of last resort model for vulnerable pupils (see Box 3.3).

> ### Box 3.3 In-house multi-agency provision to support vulnerable pupils
>
> The centre supported the individual needs of pupils through bespoke packages of provision, intervention, alternative curriculum and pathways, generally delivered on site with little external provision commissioned. The centre had access to a range of external agencies including social services, CAMHS, Youth Offending Teams (YOT) and domestic abuse-related provision to support the whole family in engaging with education.
>
> > We are multi-agency based within the centre – we have a number of partners working with us. There's always someone we can get hold of if we can't deliver the appropriate support ourselves in house. We will bring in external partners. We don't commission a lot of commercial providers, but we do have a lot of support from a network of partners and agencies.
> >
> > (Deputy head teacher)
>
> Data gathering and monitoring, including initial home visits by staff, underpinned the approach to ensure that the needs of the pupil, and often those of the wider family, were understood at the onset to act as the basis for constructing the most suitable package of support.
>
> (IOE and NFER, 2014: 54–5)

Common features of successful LSUs include:

- Well-organized learning environments;
- A varied programme of activities with a good balance between teaching and curriculum programmes and activities to support emotional and behavioural needs; this may include giving attention to improve pupils' literacy;
- Support offered to help pupils to develop better learning strategies;
- Clear entry and exit criteria;
- Thorough assessment of pupils;
- Systematic monitoring and evaluation;
- Effective liaison between the in-school centre manager, class teachers, parents and outside agencies; and
- Young people able to return to the LSU if they need further support and as a drop-in facility.

(Hallam and Rogers, 2008: 202)

Timetable flexibility

Flexible approaches to the school timetable, particularly around the subjects students find difficult, has been identified as especially effective for pupils who have had attendance difficulties (Nuttall and Woods, 2013). In the School Exclusion Trial (IOE and NFER, 2014) minor alterations to the school timetable were made to support pupils at risk of exclusion in a number of schools. In one unit for pupils at risk of exclusion, the lessons started later than those in the main school, allowing pupils time to settle into the school day.

In another school, young people with attendance issues could spend time in a specialist in-school support centre and return gradually to their main school timetable. Initially, they would identify their best lessons: the ones that drew on their strengths. This was followed by a tailored programme of phasing back until they were attending all of their lessons. This flexible arrangement seemed to be working well for the pupils. For instance, one girl had had a managed move (see the following section) into the school and would not attend PE lessons. Initially, she spent her PE time in the centre, but gradually returned to all PE lessons as a result of the support that she received.

Managed moves

Managed moves, first introduced by the *Social Inclusion: Pupil Support* document (DfEE, 1999), set out a process for reintegrating pupils to a new setting prior to schools reaching the point of permanent exclusion. Subsequent guidance (DCSF, 2004; 2010) positioned managed moves as an alternative to permanent exclusion. Reasons for why a managed move might be appropriate included instances when a school could no longer continue to educate and support a child because of their behaviour or in the case of irretrievable breakdown in relationships. Students could then be transferred to another school or an alternative educational setting.

All secondary schools were expected to be working in partnership to develop clear protocols for managed moves and hard to place young people (DCSF, 2010). The concept of managed moves, whereby students were transitioned from one school to another, offered young people a carefully planned route to secure education that took account of the student's needs (Abdelnoor, 2007). Successful managed moves can enable young people to move from a state of school disengagement to a more constructive sense of self (Bagley, 2013).

Consultation is a key concept of managed moves. Managed moves are voluntary and involve the parent/carer and the student in the decision-making process. They require secondary schools to work in partnership to find appropriate school places for students. This means that all schools involved have to work collaboratively, display trust in the judgement of the others and share responsibility for taking students from another school. Practices have varied between schools. In some, managed moves have been set up informally between head teachers and consist of a reciprocal exchange of disruptive students, whereas in others there has been a more formal and closely monitored process (OCC, 2012). There are concerns that managed moves seem to be subject to no regulation and barely any statutory guidance (CSJ, 2011). Evidence from head teachers has indicated that tensions can arise when some schools are more willing than others to take disengaged students as a managed move. Instances have been reported where parents and students have not been fully involved in the decision-making process, where managed moves operated as one of the ways some schools unofficially excluded students by offering the move under threat of a permanent exclusion, and where the managed move may not be in the best interest of the young person (OCC, 2012).

In the School Exclusion Trial (IOE and NFER, 2014), findings from the interviews and case studies drew attention to increased transparency and more rigorous processes in the use of managed moves in trial schools. In particular, this related to collaborative ways of working in which professionals, including head teachers, would meet on a regular basis to consider the appropriate support for young people (see Box 3.4). The regularity of partnership meetings and the transparency of processes contributed to the success of managed moves. Trial schools accepted a significantly higher proportion of students as the result of managed moves, and had significantly fewer students under consideration for moving out than did the comparison schools.

In one local authority, the head teachers from the 22 schools in the trial attended a monthly meeting, with the local authority officer from Pupil Access also in attendance. The officer circulated a list of requests for managed moves before the meeting. The names of all the pupils to be considered were placed on a spreadsheet with data covering the last three years. Pupils who were colour-coded red had been permanently excluded, yellow was a pending case, and green was for moves through the In Year

Fair Access arrangements. This level of detail and transparency meant that all the schools were listed and it was clear which schools had accepted managed move students and how many over time.

> BOX 3.4 TRANSPARENCY OF THE MANAGED MOVE PROCESS
> In one area partnership, managed moves were seen as the first course of action where there had been problems. Within the partnership, head teachers agreed between them to take a pupil in a managed move. Initially this would be for a six-week trial. If the first six weeks were successful then there would be a further six weeks with a review. If this was also successful the pupil would remain in the new school. As all head teachers were involved in the discussions about managed moves, everyone was aware of which schools had taken pupils: this in itself increased accountability.
>
> (IOE and NFER, 2014: 90)

Endnote

Interventions for young people at risk of disengagement in secondary school can make a difference and enable them to re-engage with their learning. For some, single-level short-term interventions might suffice to make a difference. For others, single-level interventions need to last longer, and for a few a range of interventions will be needed. Where young people have more complex needs, a personalized combination of interventions will be key to improvement in outcomes – in contrast to notions of a one-size-fits-all conceptualization of providing support.

Early identification is crucial to supporting the needs of young people at risk of disengagement. Schools that have strategies to meet these needs in-house, including specialist centres to support vulnerable students, can contribute to re-engagement. Strong pastoral support structures are essential. Where schools are involved in managed moves, strong collaboration and transparent communication within partnerships is key.

Chapter summary

In-school support for young people at risk of disengagement may be provided for individuals or groups, and can involve support from a single adult or, where young people have more complex needs, from an in-house specialist student support centre.

For some young people the best pathway might be a managed move to another setting.

Successful support depends on:

- early intervention when issues or difficulties first emerge
- clear criteria for the effective identification of young people at risk of disengagement
- thorough assessment of the needs of the young people, so that interventions are tailored to their needs
- opportunities for young people to talk through their problems and develop a range of coping strategies
- the provision of a safe, caring environment
- flexibility of provision, whether in relation to the school timetable or easy access to a centre when difficulties arise during the school day
- an ethos where young people feel valued and have opportunities to achieve success.

Chapter 4

Further education, vocational education and training

This chapter considers how FE colleges contribute to engaging young people with learning and training. Many young people entering FE have experienced educational failure and FE is seen as a last chance to re-engage with education. This chapter explores the educational ethos within colleges, the role of vocational education and apprenticeships in re-engaging young people, the challenges associated with 14- to 16-year-olds attending FE, and the opportunities provided by entrepreneurship. Case studies are given of innovative practice.

Context

Institutions such as FE colleges in England, community colleges in the US, and technical and further education (TAFE) institutions in Australia offer young people who have had poor educational experiences a second chance. In addition to supporting them to gain qualifications and improve their economic prospects, these institutions play a pivotal role in promoting social and educational inclusion. In England, it is not unusual for learners in FE to have a chequered past in terms of their formal education: for some, FE is seen as their last chance before they drop out of education and training entirely (Ofsted, 2014a). In Australia, the TAFE sector is the main public provider of second-chance options through pre-vocational or foundation skills programmes that enable early school leavers to gain qualifications equivalent to those attained at secondary school (Lamb, 2011).

While the range of programmes offered in these colleges is broad, the high level of vocational education and training (VET) can be particularly attractive to students who are at risk of disengagement or are returning to education after a period of dropout. Those who are at risk of disengagement from education particularly benefit from learning in a more adult environment than their school's. Attending college offers the opportunity to mix with older, more mature students who can potentially act as role models (Canduela *et al.*, 2010).

Internationally, VET systems play a critical role in strengthening countries' capacity to deal with rapidly changing labour-market conditions (OECD, 2013a). Many OECD countries have developed policies to improve and expand VET programmes at the upper secondary and post-secondary non-tertiary levels in order to equip young people with the skills the labour market demands. Despite the different environment and the increased VET offer, maintaining the engagement of students who are at risk of disengagement from education does present challenges. Dropout rates are quite high in apprenticeship and pre-apprenticeship programmes in England, France and Germany, for example, and in foundation skills courses in Australia.

Further education provision: An international perspective

In the UK, the post-16 education and training landscape is diverse. There are school sixth forms, sixth form colleges, general FE colleges, 16–19 academies, special post-16 institutions, and vocational learning and training providers in the private or voluntary sector. The range of study options is broad and includes AS/A-levels, vocational qualifications, apprenticeships, traineeships, supported internships and bespoke packages of learning. The main focus of the provision is VET.

FE colleges in England cater for more 16- to 18-year-olds than schools. During 2014–15, 834,000 16- to 18-year-olds studied in colleges compared to 438,000 students in maintained schools and academy sixth forms (AoC, 2015). A higher proportion of students attending colleges are from a disadvantaged background than those in sixth form colleges. During 2014–15, ethnic minority students made up 20 per cent of students in colleges, compared with 15 per cent of the general population. Among 16- to 18-year-olds, 16 per cent of college students were eligible for and claiming free school meals at age 15, compared to 9 per cent in maintained school sixth forms and academies (AoC, 2015).

VET in Australia is delivered by approximately 4,600 registered training organizations (RTOs), encompassing TAFE institutes, universities, secondary schools, private training providers, enterprises, industry organizations, community-based providers and other government organizations. The VET sector is an alternative environment for young people disaffected with the school system and has a specific role in the provision of foundation skills for those without a school certificate or low levels of literacy and numeracy (Skills Australia, 2010). As public providers, TAFE institutes are required to respond to the needs of young people disengaged from education and training, such as early school leavers and those who are unemployed and unskilled (Thomas and Hillman, 2010). Particular challenges arise in supporting indigenous students, who have experienced multiple and cumulative disadvantage. TAFE institutions and adult and community colleges offer certificates in general education, ranging from a Certificate I in Access to Work and Training through to the Year 12 equivalent Tertiary Preparation Certificate.

Community colleges in the US, of which there are over 1,000, provide education for non-traditional students. Many learners are the first generation to attend college. Admission to the two-year programme is not defined by ability or selection, although some courses need evidence of prior qualifications appropriate to the level of study. Community colleges have a specific goal to meet the needs of the region, whether this be in relation to skills, liberal arts or literacy (Boggs, 2010). In rural areas, community colleges serve as a cultural centre, as well as being the primary post-secondary education and training resource.

The ethos of further education

FE colleges and work-based training providers are more likely than schools to be able to offer specialist facilities within a real life setting as well as staff with experience of industry, both of which can help to engage young people and enable them to see the relevance of their learning (Canduela *et al.*, 2010; O'Donnell *et al.*, 2006). FE colleges offer a different environment from schools. Young people seem to appreciate the more relaxed and adult atmosphere and the more informal approach of the staff, who are called by their first names. While not all young people in FE are disengaged from education, many practices within the sector seek to support and foster re-engagement, in light of the overall levels of disadvantage among the learners. Curricula programmes that are vocational and practical clearly offer direct links to skill development and employment, and this facilitates student engagement (Attwood *et al.*, 2003; McGregor and Mills, 2012).

The range of support services – the pastoral care, career counselling, individual planning and support – all contribute to engaging students who are at risk (Brown and North, 2010). This level of individual support is exemplified in the approach taken to case management in Australia to assist disadvantaged students with additional or complex support needs to enter VET and maintain and complete their studies before moving on to further study or employment (Barnett, 2012). The focus is on providing a wrap-around service that removes the barriers to engagement. In the UK, FE makes a substantial commitment to students with learning difficulties and disabilities (see Box 7.4 in Chapter 7). Many of these students gain support to achieve success in mainstream programmes, but, for others, specially designed programmes are delivered. Foundation programmes for challenged students, whether they have learning needs or are returners to study, form a considerable part of the college workload.

Being in an adult environment that provides flexibility and autonomy and where respectful adult relationships are developed among the staff and students encourages young people to attend class (Harkin, 2006; McGregor and Mills, 2012). The culture and ethos of FE institutions is essentially responsive to the students' backgrounds and needs (Leach *et al.*, 2014; Zepke and Leach, 2010).

Vocational education and training

Vocational qualifications are important for young people at risk of disengagement from education (Burgess and Rodger, 2010; Gutherson *et al.*, 2011). They enhance engagement with learning, improve personal and social skills, and offer greater understanding of the world of work. Vocationally-oriented pathways can encourage young people to remain in or return to formal education.

In many countries, including the UK and Canada, vocational education has been an undervalued part of the education system. Writing in England, Swift and Fisher (2010: 207) refer to 'the ambivalent status surrounding vocational education', which, they argue, may deter ambitious students from entering the sector at 16 but, more importantly, may depress the levels of motivation for students who are at risk of disengagement. The aspirations of learners in FE tend to be lower than those of students who continue their studies in school sixth forms (Baird *et al.*, 2012).

Vocational programmes combine work-based and classroom learning and equip young people with the skills employers need. In Denmark, students alternate between periods spent at a training placement, most often in an enterprise, with periods of college-based learning. The work setting offers opportunities to acquire practical skills on up-to-date equipment while learning from trainers who are familiar with the most recent technologies and working methods. Students are able to develop soft skills in a real-world environment. The classroom setting provides more theoretical knowledge, broader employability skills, and foundation skills of literacy and numeracy where these need to be strengthened.

Many countries have introduced programmes to support young people in accessing VET. In Germany, pre-training schemes assist young people with low qualifications in accessing apprenticeships. Finland offers a Career Start programme for young people to explore different career opportunities (see Box 4.1).

> ## Box 4.1 Finland: Career Start programme
> The Career Start programme in Finland is aimed at young people who have dropped out of school or are unsure of their career direction. The programme enables them to try out different vocational routes and courses, visit work and training places and develop study, vocational and life skills. Professional career guidance enables young people to explore different career and job opportunities before selecting their study or employment route. Programmes last from 20 to 40 weeks, depending on the needs of the individual, and students are able to move from courses offering preparatory instruction to those leading to certification. Each young person designs their own development plan with support from their tutor, and activities are tailored to individual needs and aspirations.
>
> (Cedefop, 2010; Hawley *et al.*, 2012)

In Australia, foundation skills courses offered by TAFE institutes have the specific goal of enabling students to acquire the literacy, numeracy and employability skills required for further study or employment (Roberts and Wignall, 2010). Most students enrolling in these courses have not completed Year 10 of secondary school and are from backgrounds associated with educational disadvantage. Foundation skills courses are offered at three levels. Certificate I courses are for students who have had interrupted schooling or experienced major barriers to their education. Certificate II and III courses are qualifications considered to be equivalent of Year 10 in school (Murray and Mitchell, 2015).

These foundation skills courses, similar to BTEC (Business and Technology Education Council) vocational qualifications in England, are assessed according to a competency model requiring students to demonstrate mastery of specific skills to complete units of assessment (see Chapter 10). The students, with the support of their teachers, practise skills and resubmit pieces of work until they reach set levels of competency. Vocational qualifications are often structured to enable students to work on units of assessment that build up to certificated assessment over time. However, there are concerns internationally that vocational qualifications lack the credibility of academic qualifications and that the qualifications obtained are at too low a level in relation to employment (Wolf, 2011). Concerns have also been expressed over the tick-box approach to assessment where students work through a demonstration of skills. Nevertheless, enabling students to have a second chance to take qualifications (Burgess and Rodger, 2010) and having a curriculum offer that enables young people to build up qualifications (GHK Consulting, 2009) can assist young people engage with education and experience success. This differs from their previous educational career, and success can help foster persistence and the development of self-confidence in their learning (Murray and Mitchell, 2015). Foundation courses have a crucial role to play in providing a bridge to higher level qualifications when students have been absent or disengaged from education.

In the US, Job Corps, a mainly residential programme for young people at risk, provides academic and work-based learning, as well as employability skills training (see Box 4.2).

Box 4.2 Job Corps US for low income young people

Job Corps in the US operates in 125 centres in 48 states, providing a residential and educational workforce training programme for economically disadvantaged young people aged 16 to 24. The typical Job Corps student is a high school dropout who reads at slightly less than the eighth grade level. Students live on Job Corps centres, which are open 24 hours a day, seven days a week. Here they learn vocational trades through a variety of methods, from hands-on instruction to job shadowing to internships. Nationally, Job Corps offers more than 100 occupations in industries including automotive, information technology, security, construction and health care. Job Corps also provides academic training, including high school diploma attainment opportunities and/or General Educational Development (GED) programmes. Job Corps is a self-paced programme. The lengths of stay vary although most stay for nine months. Classes are small with dedicated teachers and most Job Corps students improve their maths and reading skills dramatically during their time on the programme. A career transition service is offered for 12 months to ensure graduates have the support system to succeed in the workplace. High levels of employer engagement mean that employers help students prepare for careers through mock interviews and internships, for example. They also assist in students' career transition from Job Corps to the workforce through mentoring and support services. Success rates are promising. In the programme year ending June 2014, 77 per cent of all Job Corps graduates were successfully placed, with 64 per cent starting careers and 13 per cent enrolling in higher education.

(NJCA, 2015)

Apprenticeships

In many industries, apprenticeships and traineeships provide the best pathway for skills development. They combine structured training for a nationally recognized qualification with employment. Apprenticeships are offered in many countries, including Australia, France, Ireland, England and the US. Some countries, such as Austria, Germany and Switzerland, have dual systems where training takes place in both private companies and vocational schools. In Germany, apprenticeships have high status and have traditionally played a significant role in training young workers. Some 60 per cent of an age cohort receives its basic vocational training in the form of an apprenticeship (Walden and Troitsch, 2011). In Australia, almost 100,000 employers, more than half of them small businesses, employ around 400,000 apprentices and trainees.

Apprenticeships are seen as a successful alternative to more formal classroom-based education and can support young people who are disengaged from education in returning to education and training (Birdwell *et al.*, 2011; Cedefop, 2010; Gracey and Kelly, 2010). Apprenticeships can ease the transition between education and work and hence offer a learning pathway for young people who are at risk of dropping out of education (OECD, 2014c). Anderson *et al.* (2010) indicate that the probability of unemployment is reduced following apprenticeship training. Given the increasing necessity for young people to have upper secondary qualifications, this is important.

In response to concerns with young people who are disengaged from education, many countries have strengthened apprenticeship programmes. Denmark introduced a new apprenticeship scheme in 2006 as part of the government strategy to reduce the number of early school leavers. Within the UK, the decision to raise the participation age to 18 has necessitated strong apprenticeship provision and government investment prioritizes the enablement of more young people to move into work and training through apprenticeships. In 2010–11, 457,200 people began an apprenticeship; of these 131,700 were young people under the age of 19. In Korea, a new apprenticeship system began in January 2014 that drew on systems in place in Australia, Germany and the UK (OECD, 2014c).

However, in many countries demand exceeds the number of available apprenticeships (Steedman, 2010; OECD, 2014c). One consequence is the tendency to offer them to young people with high educational qualifications, to the disadvantage of young people disengaged from education. In Norway, the lack of places means that young people have no alternative but to complete an additional year in school. For students at risk of disengagement from education, an additional year at school may be particularly problematic, since they may well have chosen the apprenticeship path for its strong vocational element.

Increasingly, countries have introduced pre-apprenticeship programmes in part to engage young people who are disengaged from education and lack the qualifications to move directly into an apprenticeship. In Ontario, Canada, pre-apprenticeship training programmes are offered by colleges, approved apprenticeship deliverers, and community agencies at various times throughout the year. Targeted at young people who may be disengaged from education, including early school leavers and unemployed/underemployed youth and adults, they support potential entrants to the apprenticeship system develop their job skills and readiness, preparing them to find work as an apprentice. There is no cost to participate in a pre-apprenticeship programme, and text books, safety equipment and tools are supplied free of charge.

In England, traineeships were implemented in August 2013. Traineeships are targeted at 16- to 24-year-olds who lack the skills or experience to be able to apply for an apprenticeship. Typically traineeships comprise work placement, work preparation, and, where necessary, support for English and maths. They may also provide mentors who act as role models, and some programmes offer support to deal with behaviour and anger management (see Box 4.3).

Box 4.3 Enabling the transition to apprenticeship programmes for young people disengaged from education
The Motive8 training programme, run by Enfield Training Services, was targeted at young people who were less likely to be engaged in learning. This included gang members, looked-after children, and young offenders. Learners might have limited qualifications, be unready for work, and lack direction.

Motive8 supported changes in attitude to behaviour, including conflict and anger management, in addition to drug and alcohol awareness. For instance, young men with behavioural difficulties were taught by mentors who were former offenders themselves.

Approximately 60 young people participated in the training programme. Destinations included apprenticeships, FE, Foundation Learning Programmes and short-term employment.

(Ofsted, 2012)

14- to 16-year-olds in further education

The number of students aged between 14 and 16 attending FE has increased in recent years in England. Currently, 33,500 14- and 15-year-olds are enrolled at a college, 2,000 of them full time and 31,500 part-time (AoC, 2015). The increase stemmed from government policy (DfES, 2002; 2003) and specific educational initiatives such as the piloting of the increased flexibility programme (IFP; beginning 2002) and the implementation of the 14–19 Diplomas (beginning 2008), both with strong vocational elements. Although both initiatives have ceased, the number of young people in FE seems likely to increase given changes in legislation coupled with the raising of the participation age to 18 in 2015. Since September 2013, FE colleges and sixth form colleges have been able to enrol, and require direct funding from the Education Funding Agency for 14- to 16-year-olds who wish to study high-quality vocational qualifications alongside general qualifications including English and maths (DfE, 2014b). Government guidance requires that, while the education may take place all around the college, there should be a designated and identifiable area or 14 to 16 centre exclusively providing education and support for these young people.

The IFP for 14- to 16-year-olds provided vocational learning opportunities. Partnerships were formed with schools, colleges and training providers, often led by one FE college. The two-year programme entailed students working towards vocational qualifications such as BTECs or vocational GCSEs for one or two days a week, while the remainder of the time was spent in school studying academic subjects. Students liked the practical approach to learning and could see connections with the programme of study and the world of work. Most of those in the first cohort of the programme continued in education or training post-16 (Golden *et al.*, 2005). The experience of working in a college environment on vocational learning made a difference. As one teacher stated:

> A lot of year 11s wouldn't have finished school if they hadn't gone on the IFP ... a lot of them are now considering college or work. Without the IFP a lot of them wouldn't be qualified or going on to FE.
>
> (O'Donnell, 2006: 50)

Box 4.4 illustrates the progression from the IFP to employment.

Promoting enterprise and entrepreneurship

A short section is included here on entrepreneurship education, since study programmes and initiatives across many countries, for example Australia, Canada and the US, are giving young people the opportunity to develop new skills and career pathways. Entrepreneurship education is seen as assisting young people to develop entrepreneurial skills, attitudes and behaviours in addition to enterprise awareness and the understanding that entrepreneurship represents a career option (Schoof, 2006). Developing an entrepreneurial attitude among young people can help them overcome barriers and develop self-confidence (European Commission, 2001). Importantly, entrepreneurship can offer young people from disadvantaged groups a pathway out of social exclusion: for young people at risk it can support transition into work (Cedefop, 2010), and may represent an alternative to formal education. Programmes to encourage or assist young people start their own businesses may be helpful for unemployed and disadvantaged young people (OECD, 2013b).

The Prince's Trust Enterprise programme (Prince's Trust, 2015a), which was established in the UK 30 years ago, helps unemployed and disadvantaged young people to explore entrepreneurial ideas and turn their business plans into reality with the help of a low-interest loan and a mentor. As part of the programme, participants attend a four-day workshop about personal goals and skills, finance, marketing and the legal structures involved in setting up a business. More individualized support follows, to help the young person develop their business plan. Those who gain approval for their business plan are then supported by an experienced business mentor for two years.

FE colleges within the UK are increasingly embedding enterprise and entrepreneurship within their curriculum offer, whether as part of the taught provision or informal activities. Barking and Dagenham College, for instance, in addition to running business start-up and entrepreneurial skills courses, has a free creative zone, the Pod (Pitch on Demand) for student entrepreneurs and local small businesses to help get ideas off the ground. Facilities include hot-desking, IT support, advice on funding, networking opportunities and business workshops. Box 4.4 provides a case study of a student who initially attended college for one day a week as part of the IFP and was able to secure employment by developing her enterprise-related skills.

> **BOX 4.4 ACHIEVING SUCCESS THROUGH DEVELOPING ENTERPRISE-RELATED SKILLS**
>
> The student gained a Level 1 hairdressing qualification while attending college as part of the 14 to 16 IFP. After this she joined the college full time and studied for a Level 2 qualification, at the same time attending a work placement one day a week. As part of the process for gaining entry to Level 3, she was required to undertake a trades test in front of several employers. At college she was involved in many cross-college and external events, and entered competitions to develop her skills. In addition to her vocational qualifications, she gained other qualifications in work skills, teamwork and work-related skills that helped her to develop enterprise-related skills and entrepreneurship capability. On leaving college she was given the chance to rent a chair in a hairdressing salon. She had the confidence to accept the opportunity.
>
> (Ofsted, 2012)

Endnote

For young people who are at risk of disengagement from education or who have left school early, the provision offered in FE colleges and similar institutions worldwide can provide a pathway back to education and training. The more relaxed atmosphere, the wider, more practical curriculum that relates directly to the world of work can help engage young people. VET that offers a curriculum of industry value is important in enabling young people disengaged from education to see the relevance of their learning. In addition, unit-based assessment approaches that place an emphasis on mastery, with the option to re-take, afford young people important opportunities to gain success in education. Central to this is the supportive relationship they enjoy with lecturers and training providers who adopt student-centred approaches to teaching and learning.

Chapter summary

FE colleges and similar institutions have an important role to play in engaging young people who are disengaged from education, and may offer a last chance for education. Educational provision in FE works well when:

- strong support mechanisms are in place to help with young people's needs
- supportive, more relaxed, relationships with teachers and lecturers are encouraged in addition to high levels of pastoral care
- young people are encouraged to follow programmes of study that are matched to their aspirations
- vocational education and training are of direct relevance to the world of work
- multiple pathways to progression exist, including foundation-level qualifications and pre-traineeships
- young people are afforded opportunities to achieve educational success.

It is important for the future that further research is undertaken in relation to the experience and progression of young people aged 14 to 16 in FE as this is currently lacking.

Chapter 5

Young people in the criminal justice system

This chapter explores educational provision for young people attending Young Offender Institutions (YOIs) or similar settings. It considers the particular issues of providing education and training in custodial settings and why education is so important for these young people. The chapter also considers the challenges that young people face when leaving custody.

Context

A young offender is a person within a certain age range who has committed a criminal offence. Young offenders worldwide are often detained in secure custodial settings that are very similar to an adult prison. The proportion of young people who are detained, the provision made for young people who have offended, the approach taken to education, and the age of criminal responsibility all vary widely from country to country. In many countries young offending accounts for a disproportionate amount of all crime (England and Wales: National Audit Office, 2010; Australia: Australian Institute of Criminology, 2011).

Young people in prison are vulnerable. Many arrive with profound disadvantage, poor educational attainment and fragmented educational histories. Overall, the educational provision for young people in the secure estate is uneven and seldom matches that of their peers in mainstream education in terms of the range of the curriculum offered or the quality and opportunities for progression. Providing education within the secure estate is extremely challenging. Issues arise from the custodial constraints imposed by the systems and processes in operation, concerns for the safety of young people, and the challenges posed in prison by gangs.

It is important that these young people are afforded high-quality education and training that meets their personal needs and their learning or employment pathways after they leave custody. Raising the educational attainment and inclusion of young people who have offended is one of the most effective means of reducing the risk factors associated with criminal behaviour.

Young offenders: the international context

There is considerable variation in the way each country approaches the incarceration of children and the age of criminal responsibility. In England, the minimum age of criminal responsibility is ten, considerably lower than in many other jurisdictions. In Scandinavian countries, the age of criminal responsibility starts at 15. In Brazil, the minimum age is 18, whereas in Mexico the minimum age is six. In the US, different states have their own responsibility for juvenile justice legislation, policies and processes. In some states, children as young as six can be held criminally responsible; in others the minimum age is 17. According to the United Nations Committee on the Rights of the Child (2007), a minimum age of criminal responsibility below the age of 12 years is not internationally acceptable.

Comparing international statistics about young offenders is difficult. There is variation in where young people are placed, for example detention centres, residential treatment facilities or even adult prisons, and in whether each type of setting is included in the statistical reports (Muncie, 2006; Elwick *et al.*, 2013). Broad comparisons can be made by considering the different rates of young people per 100,000 who are in custodial settings. In Scandinavian countries, few young offenders are imprisoned. In Finland, the rate is 0.2 per 100,000 compared with 31 in Australia and 295 in the US (Murphy *et al.*, 2010).

Countries adopt different perspectives on juvenile justice. In Norway, provision centres on welfare and the needs of young people (Hazel, 2008). In New Zealand, the youth justice system is largely based on the idea of restorative justice. Historically, England and Wales have had one of the highest youth populations in custody in Europe (Jacobson *et al.*, 2010; Elwick *et al.*, 2013). The total number of children in custody, both sentenced and remanded, peaked at 3,175 in October 2002 (Jacobsen *et al.*, 2010). In August 2014, 1,068 young people under the age of 18 were held in custody, 741 in YOIs, 240 in secure training centres, and 87 in secure children's homes. At this time there were 48 children aged 14 and under in the secure estate (Prison Reform Trust, 2014). In the US, approaches to young offenders rely heavily on incarceration as a punishment. In 2014, there were more than 2,500 people sentenced to die in prison for crimes committed before they had turned 18 (Rovner,

2014). The US is the only country in the world that sentences children to life without parole.

These different international perspectives on youth justice impact on custodial rates of young offenders, with high custody rates associated with justice-based systems and lower rates with welfare-based systems (Murphy *et al.*, 2010). These perspectives impact on the nature and type of educational provision offered during custody and the steps taken to enable young people to reintegrate into society after their sentence.

Characteristics of young offenders

Young people within the criminal justice system are not a homogenous group. They are, however, among the most vulnerable and troubled youth in society and often present with complex health, social and emotional needs, which may have arisen from experiences of peer pressure and gang-related activities, poor parenting, family rejection, emotional trauma, violence and abuse, and drug and alcohol abuse (SEU, 2002; Farrington and Welsh, 2006; Bradley, 2009; Jacobson *et al.*, 2010; McCord *et al.*, 2012).

A high proportion of young offenders will have been excluded from school at some stage (SEU, 2002; Tye, 2009). In Australia, 84 per cent of male young offenders and 93 per cent of female young offenders had left school by Year 10 and had a history of truanting and suspension before that (Sacher, 2006). In England and Wales, 86 per cent of boys and all the girls in a Youth Justice Board survey said they had been excluded from school. More than a third of the boys (37 per cent) and nearly two-thirds of the girls (65 per cent) said they had not been at school since they were 14 (Kennedy, 2013).

Young offenders tend to show levels of underachievement and learning disability. Young men are around 9 times and young women around 15 times more likely to be unqualified compared with non-offenders of a similar age (Machin *et al.*, 2010). Young offenders internationally often have poor skills in language, literacy and numeracy (Hurry *et al.*, 2010; Talbot, 2010).

Internationally, some groups of young people are disproportionally represented in the criminal justice system. In Northern Ireland, young people in care, or who have been in care, are significantly more likely to experience prison than their peers (Include Youth, 2011). In Australia, indigenous youths are overrepresented. In New South Wales, for instance, they made up 52 per cent of 10- to 17-year-olds in juvenile institutions in 2005, although indigenous people represent only 2–3 per cent of the total population (Murphy *et al.*, 2010). In the US in 2011, the residential placement for black youth was more than 4.5 times the rate for white youth (Hockenberry, 2014).

The importance of education for young offenders

Learning provision is important for prisoners of all ages but especially important for young offenders, as many would ordinarily be in full-time education. Internationally education and training are seen as one pathway out of re-offending. Analysis by the Centre for Economic Performance (Machin *et al.*, 2010) supports the idea that improving the educational attainment of marginalized adults can help reduce crime. Schuller (2009) identified economic, social and moral rationales for improving lifelong learning for offenders, and evidence from the US supports the view that adult prisoners participating in educational programmes have lower rates of recidivism than non-participants (Davis *et al.*, 2013).

Re-offending rates are higher for under-18-year-olds than for their adult counterparts. In England and Wales, 73 per cent of young offenders released from custody in 2011 re-offended within 12 months (Ministry of Justice, 2013) compared to a re-offending rate of 47.2 per cent by adults (Ministry of Justice, 2012). In Scotland, 60 per cent of 16- and 17-year-olds sentenced to a YOI in 2009 were reconvicted within two years of release (Scottish Government, 2012). Good educational provision while in custody is seen as critical in enabling young offenders to have the best chance of succeeding when they return to the community (Ministry of Justice, 2013).

Right to education

Regardless of where young people are detained, international agreements exist about the provision of education. Rule 38 of The United Nations Rules for the Protection of Juveniles Deprived of their Liberty (United Nations, 1990) states that 'every juvenile of compulsory school age has the right to education suited to his or her needs and abilities and designed to prepare him or her for return to society'. Rule 39 stipulates that 'juveniles above compulsory school age who wish to continue their education should be permitted and encouraged to do so, and every effort should be made to provide them with access to appropriate educational programmes'. Young offenders of compulsory school age are to be denied education only as a last resort, and, in relation to young offenders of statutory school age, inadequate educational facilities could amount to a breach of Article 2 of the second protocol of the Convention.

Places of detention should maximize young people's chances of rehabilitation and integration into society (Article 40(1) of the United Nations Convention on the Rights of the Child, 1989) by providing an environment where they will be assisted through education and other programmes to make better choices about their lives during and after custody. Rule 38 of the Havana Rules (United Nations, 1990) draws attention to the importance of ensuring that education is provided by qualified teachers and, critically, that education 'is integrated with the education system of the country so that, after release, juveniles may continue their education without difficulty'.

Educational provision in the secure estate: an overview

Practitioners working with young people in secure settings are often confronted with learners whose previous experiences of education present a barrier. They may feel let down by their previous experiences of school or have had extensive periods of absence, or have dropped out. They may have experienced educational failure. Despite these challenges, evidence suggests that educational practitioners working in prisons are often motivated by a desire to make a difference and improve the life chances of people who have been failed by the system. Many educators enter this work out of altruism and this suggests a highly committed workforce (Rogers *et al.*, 2014b).

Young people themselves value education. In a consultation about developing a strategy for the secure estate, most young people in the focus groups said they wanted education to support their return to the community. They wanted to gain skills in custody that would better equip them on release. Specifically, they wanted better ways of working for GCSEs, coupled with college placements when returning to the community. They valued vocational courses leading to apprenticeships or employment (Glover *et al.*, 2012). Most of them felt that the education they received was not equipping them with the education or life skills that would help them find work and avoid further offending.

In England and Wales, young people are expected to take part weekly in 15 hours of education plus an additional 10 hours of purposeful activity. There is a mandatory requirement to provide at least 15 hours of education weekly to those below school-leaving age (HM Government, 2000, Rule 38). Formal education and vocational training are offered. Subjects include ICT, art, graphic design, media, personal and social development, and business enterprise. Most qualifications start at Level 1 with progression to Level 2, although few take Level 2 qualifications. YOIs also offer basic English and maths, beginning at entry level. Vocational provision includes barbering, brickwork, carpentry, catering, computer workshop, construction, gardening, hospitality, motorcycle maintenance, motor vehicle work, painting and decorating, performing arts, radio production and multimedia, waste management and recycling (Hurry *et al.*, 2012). In addition, young people may undertake work experience such as kitchen work, wing cleaning, garden maintenance, and laundry, and gain qualifications in these areas.

Variability in educational provision is seen across the UK. Provision at Woodlands Juvenile Justice Centre in Northern Ireland is well regarded. Inspectors observed that young people were required to attend education, class sizes were small, initial and progress educational assessments were performed in a timely fashion, and programmes included a range of vocational and occupational skills as well as standard curricula (CJINI, 2011). In contrast, provision at Hydebank Wood Young Offenders Centre was poor. Activity places were insufficient and those available were poorly used. Levels of attainment and accreditation were too low, particularly in literacy and numeracy. Too few young offenders were engaged in challenging work activities, and the opportunities for them to gain work-related qualifications were poor (CJINI, 2013). The same variability is seen in England, as illustrated by the recent inspection report for Hindley (HMCIP, 2014a), where Ofsted's assessment about the learning and skills and work provision was good in all categories, whereas at Feltham (HMCIP, 2014b) all areas required improvement.

The challenges of providing education in the secure estate

Attendance issues

Attendance rates vary across YOIs. Even though education is mandatory up to the age of 18 in England and Wales, participation rates in education or training for those on remand is low, approximately 40 per cent (Hurry *et al.*, 2012). Young people can be absent from education for reasons such as sickness or because they are not eligible for provision due to behavioural issues. Staff have to work with the churn and the unpredictable attendance of young people, who are dependent on prison officers for their rooms to be unlocked and to be accompanied from the dormitory wing to the education premises. Where prison and education staff work together to prioritize attendance and where education is regarded as important, the chances of re-offending can be reduced (see Box 5.1).

BOX 5.1 PROMOTING ATTENDANCE

In one YOI where the prison and education staff worked together to prioritise attendance in classes, achievement was high. This was attained by focusing on fully integrated timetables, to which two staff are dedicated, and by prioritising the way in which allocation to courses took place, which involves four members of staff. Additionally, in this case, there is a prison-wide ethos that everyone takes responsibility for ensuring that education, training and purposeful activity are given a high status. The ethos is 'don't exclude', so that even if a prisoner is sick or confined to the wing the teachers must supply work to be done. Attendance in the library is closely monitored. One of the factors that enables this to happen is the close relationship between the Head of Learning and Skills and the Education Manager who work together on a daily basis.

(Hurry *et al.*, 2012: 21)

The length of stay means that there is insufficient time for young offenders to achieve qualifications. In England and Wales, the average length of a custodial sentence for young offenders is 85 days (Ministry of Justice, 2014). In Scotland, the average sentence length is between two to four years: sentences range from six months to life. Accordingly, some YOIs offer short units of qualifications to enable young offenders to gain accreditation before they leave.

Behaviour management

Behaviour management is an issue in many YOIs, especially where there is conflict between gangs. Successful approaches to behaviour management in mainstream education are based on the consistent application of a well-developed behaviour policy with clear rewards and consequences, that is understood by all (Hallam and Rogers, 2008). The same applies to the secure estate. As in mainstream education, young people might occasionally need to be removed from the classroom environment for a short period of time: it is essential that incidents are managed fairly and that they can return to their lessons.

Teaching needs to promote active learning and engage the students. Often teaching sessions are three hours long, so need to be clearly structured into chunked activities that take account of learners' concentrations spans. As one education manager in a YOI commented: 'Incidents of violence are high – there is a need for different teaching approaches that are active, interactive and participative, that will take care of concentration and relate to their interests' (Rogers *et al.*, 2014a: 192).

Young offenders, like those in alternative educational provision, often fail to see the relevance of the curriculum to their needs and interests (see Chapters 9, 10 and 11). This can often be the case particularly for functional skills, if the approach taken is not integrated with the wider curricula offer. The example in Box 5.2 demonstrates how lessons can be made more interactive and engaging to maintain the learners' interest. They also gain from opportunities to develop their self-confidence.

Box 5.2 Use of technology to engage learners

English and maths lessons were well planned. Good use was made of interactive technology to involve young people, for example in a mathematics session young people could check if their answers were correct. In other sessions, interactive quizzes were used as starter activities and in an ICT [Information and Communication Technology] session a video was used to support understanding of a practical activity. Learning sessions provided good opportunities for young people to develop their listening, communication and reading skills, to increase their confidence and to work with their peers.

(HMCIP, 2014a: 54)

Security issues

In YOIs, security issues impinge on the education offer (Rogers *et al.*, 2014a). For instance, some courses are restricted because of the danger presented by resources that could be used as weapons. Science, for example, is problematic due to the need to use potentially dangerous substances and chemicals, so it is seldom offered in YOIs and internet access is generally unavailable. Security requirements also mean that scissors have to be plastic, for example, and latex cannot be used because of potential allergic reactions.

Some educational providers find creative solutions to these challenges. In one YOI, almost 50 per cent of the boys were not allowed to receive vocational training because of security risks, but project-based learning was developed in conjunction with the local authority to support those who were not eligible for vocational work (see Box 5.3). Project work was seen as useful, interesting, and related to learners' lives after release; it was also seen as offering them the opportunity to acquire skills to raise their employability. It often had the added benefits of being practical and hands-on (Rogers *et al.*, 2014a).

> BOX 5.3 PROVISION FOR YOUNG PEOPLE NOT ELIGIBLE FOR VOCATIONAL WORK
>
> The intention was to offer students excluded from vocational training something more practical than the more formal English and maths. A range of topics was covered, such as house of the future and job of the future, offering scope for creativity and imagination in an area of interest to students and opportunities for embedded learning of functional skills. For example, for house of the future, students designed their own house, using Excel work skills and IT. Design would involve measuring, costing and writing, as well as creative design. Students would design rooms one at a time, e.g. kitchen, bathroom or games room, but this tended to become rather mechanical and repetitive, so teachers developed the activities to open up possibilities, with themes like save the planet, houses of the past and the future, mood boards and style of living.
>
> (Hurry *et al.*, 2012: 14)

A holistic approach to education

Affording young people opportunities for educational success empowers them and is a necessary step to progression. As well as achieving, developing their learning skills and self-image is important, although this often goes unrecognized. This holistic learning approach is perceived as valuable for several reasons. Many young offenders have a low level of educational attainment and have a poor view of the statutory education they received. Changing this attitude and their views of learning is important for their future development. Many young offenders have mental and physical health issues and disabilities, often accompanied by low self-confidence, so providing the context in a classroom to raise a learner's self-esteem is essential. Young people with low self-esteem and self-confidence are unlikely to learn well or be able to perform well in the world of work or training after release.

The example in Box 5.4 describes a raptor project in one YOI in England where the strengths and skills of prison staff were used to offer an enriched curriculum to young offenders who lacked self-esteem and confidence.

BOX 5.4 RAPTOR PROJECT FOR YOUNG BOYS

Boys were involved in the full range of activities from the outset, preparing the site for the birds, building the sheds, laying paths. They had to read up on how to rear the birds, learn how to care for them and how to fly them. Taking them out to display them to the general public involved another set of skills and responsibility and gave boys the opportunity to perform for their families too. All this learning was in an interesting and exciting context. One boy who had not handled birds of prey before remarked 'I was scared of the birds at first. But once you get bitten by one you soon get used to it.' He hand reared a kestrel to which he was much attached. 'It sits on my shoulder.' Another young man, recently released, wants to work with birds, and his YOT [Youth Offending Team] are helping him to apply to a zoo.

(Hurry *et al.*, 2012: 25)

Achievement and progression

Too much work in YOIs lacks sufficient challenge and is offered at low levels, limiting opportunities for progression for young people both while in custody and after their release (Rogers *et al.*, 2014a). In one YOI, young people developed good skills in brickwork and produced complex structures, but these were not accredited above Level 1. By contrast, another YOI afforded for more advanced learners opportunities to practise high-level skills in brickwork and painting and decorating.

It is difficult for YOIs to be able to deliver GCSE qualifications. If young people transfer in during their GCSEs, efforts are made to support them as much as possible. In some cases, the YOI enabled a learner to sit a GCSE exam, but could not deliver full tuition in that subject. While staff tried their hardest to accommodate learners wishing to take GSCEs, emphasis was placed on those who had perceived skills deficits. Most of the time, energy and resources were taken up with mandated provision (Hurry *et al.*, 2012).

Where staff have high expectations of their students and use individual learning plans effectively for planning, setting targets the young people themselves use to demonstrate progress, progression will be successful.

Resettlement: Education and training

The reintegration of young people into the community after a period in custody is challenging (Dyer, 2014). While transitions can be difficult for many (see Chapter 8), for those moving from the secure estate these challenges are acute. These are adolescents and in the middle of many developmental transitions from child to adult status. They have fewer opportunities while making this transition to adulthood than peers who have not been removed from their communities. Most of those leaving custody are vulnerable and many have complex and wide-ranging problems. Multiple sources of support may be needed – from families, employment, and training agencies, and with accommodation and housing. The focus is on education and training.

The approach to young offenders taken in different countries impacts on the provision for their resettlement. In Canada, where the main focus is on rehabilitation, every period of custody is followed by a period of supervision in the community. All young people sent to prison are also given a specified community supervision sentence (Department of Justice, Canada 2013). Prior to and while serving this sentence, they are assigned a youth worker who works with them to plan for their reintegration, which can include periods of reintegration leave in preparation for their return to the community.

The experience of being in a YOI is highly disruptive to education (Wilson, 2010). Lack of access to education, training, and employment and the lack of appropriate provision are significant barriers to changing the behaviour and expectations of young people who offend or who are likely to offend (Ofsted, 2010b). When schools, colleges, and providers of work-based learning do not understand the youth offending system, it is harder for young people to reintegrate into mainstream education and training. The use of different exam boards and different subject choices together with poor arrangements for sending on information about previous study and achievement add to the lack of continuity (Ofsted, 2010b). Support for transition into the community can, however, work well (see Box 5.5).

> **Box 5.5 Support for resettlement**
>
> A boy aged 15 had benefited from a highly effective assessment of his needs and the actions that needed to be taken to help him achieve his aspirations of working in the construction industry on his release from a secure children's home. Work towards resettlement was happening from the early stages of his sentence. His time in the secure children's home was used to enable him to gain useful work experience as well as appropriate qualifications.
>
> When he began the community-based part of his sentence, he joined a construction company and undertook further training and qualifications. The youth offending team and the secure children's home remained in contact with him and provided support when needed.
>
> (Ofsted, 2010b: 12–13)

Endnote

There are many examples of good educational provision for young people detained in secure institutions that facilitate progression and resettlement. However, the prison curriculum struggles to match the range of educational options available in the community. Even though the learners are available, attendance levels can be poor and it is hard to provide a rich curriculum of education and training matched to students' interests and abilities. There remains a lack of research about educational provision for young people: their perceptions of their educational provision, and reintegration and the impact that education may have.

Young people in custody are particularly vulnerable. Education is one way of enabling them to make different choices, but only if the provision is of high quality and they are fully supported to progress their education when they return to the community.

Chapter summary

Effective educational provision in the secure estate is characterized by:

- high expectations of learners
- tailored curriculum offer to meet the needs of individuals
- a holistic approach to education that encompasses the development of self-confidence, self-esteem and a positive view of education in the learners
- interactive approaches to teaching and learning in which learners see the relevance of their study to work and employment.

Challenges remain in relation to:

- the narrow curricula offer
- lack of progression to higher level qualifications, with too many young people insufficiently challenged by the work they are undertaking
- the effective integration of English and maths into an applied curriculum.

Effective resettlement in relation to education involves:

- early preparation for release, in which the young offender is fully involved
- continuity in educational opportunities and the presence of the same key worker throughout
- sustained support after release
- coordination of services to ensure that the needs of the young person are met.

Chapter 6

Not in education, employment or training

An increasing concern across many developed countries is the rise in the number of young people described as NEET. This chapter explores the emergence and use of the term NEET, the precursors to becoming NEET, the characteristics of those who are NEET, the consequences of being NEET, policy responses to NEET, and initiatives to support young people to return to mainstream education, training or employment.

Context

The term NEET emerged in the UK in the 1980s. Since then, young people encompassed by the term NEET have attracted much attention from policymakers, governments, and the international press. This is because, in addition to the personal costs to the individual, there are wider costs to the public purse in relation to reduced economic productivity, tax, healthcare, benefit payments and crime. In an attempt to tackle the NEET problem, many governments have set targets to reduce the number of NEET. Within this context, NEET has become an indicator to measure the unemployed and the inactive, enabling comparison between countries.

In the same way that disengagement from education can be thought of as being on a continuum, the term NEET encompasses a spectrum of vulnerability, educational and economic disadvantage and disengagement. Many young people have a period of being NEET. They could be taking time out from work or study or seeking job opportunities or training programmes that are better suited to their aspirations. Even those who are NEET for six months may not face significant educational or employment disadvantage. At the far end of the spectrum, though, are the young people who have multiple and complex barriers to education, employment and training. These young people often require long-term specialist intervention programmes to assist them in improving their life chances and it is they who warrant most attention.

The emergence and use of the term NEET

In the UK during the 1970s and early 1980s, there was a need to establish an indicator to capture young people who were not employed, in education or in training. This was in response to the growing concern about these young people, given the collapse of the youth labour market, increasing rates of youth underemployment and crime, and a number of inner city disturbances (Haywood *et al.*, 2008). A pivotal study in Wales (Istance *et al.*, 1994) used the term Status Zer0 (later changed to Status A) to refer to young people aged 16–18 not in education, training, or employment and not covered in any of the main categories of labour market status. Status Zer0 in this context was a technical term that originated from career services' records. Status 1 referred to young people in education, Status 2 to those in training, and Status 3 to those in employment.

The term NEET was recognized in 1999 with the publication of the *Bridging the Gap* report (SEU, 1999). The term rapidly gained importance beyond the UK and similar definitions were adopted in almost all EU member states. Other countries, such as Japan, Hong Kong, New Zealand and Taiwan developed their own definitions (Eurofound, 2012). NEET is now seen to contain a variety of subgroups ranging from young people who are conventionally unemployed to those who are unavailable for work because of family responsibilities (Eurofound, 2012). The NEET group also contains young people who are not actively seeking work.

Criticisms of the term NEET

Early definitions of the term were criticized as implying that young people categorized as NEET were a homogenous group and that all who were labelled NEET were subject to the same risks and challenges. It is now recognized that the NEET category is broad and includes young people in diverse situations. Some are actively seeking work, some are not seeking work, and some are unable to work. Those not seeking work may have other responsibilities, such as caring for other children, or parents, some may have health problems, and some may be volunteering or taking time off to travel. Being NEET also depends on the employment situation. So we should not interpret the NEET status as being negative for all young people, especially since the label NEET defines young people by what they are not, rather than what they are (Yates and Payne, 2006; Simmons and Thompson, 2011).

Definitions often ignore the level of control an individual has in exercising choice over their situation (Furlong, 2006). Some make an active choice to become classified as NEET so they can pursue other hobbies or interests. Others may be the only carer for a parent and have no choice. Some have difficult personal circumstances, including caring responsibilities, domestic violence, youth offending, illness or learning disabilities (Simmons and Thompson, 2011).

A further issue, particularly when international comparisons are made, is that global statistics on NEET often mask regional and local variation, which in turn can reflect huge variation in employment levels. Within England, overall rates for NEETs are higher in the North and in the West Midlands (Allen *et al.*, 2012).

The approach taken in this chapter is not to pathologize young people termed NEET. While it is agreed that conceptions of NEET may be flawed, the term has kept the issues of youth unemployment on the political agenda. This broad concept has drawn attention to the multifaceted nature of young people's problems and initiated consideration of patterns of vulnerability of young people rather than continuing to marginalize them by the adoption of the inactive label (Eurofound, 2012; Furlong, 2006).

NEETs: An international perspective

The age categories that countries focus on in relation to the NEET group vary. In the UK, the focus is predominantly on teenagers, as in New Zealand. In Japan, the NEET group is defined as people aged 15–34 years who are not in the labour force, attending school or housekeeping (OECD, 2008a). In Korea, NEET refers to a similar age cohort but relates to those who have left school, who are not preparing to enter a company, do not have a job, do not have family responsibilities (or children), and are not married (OECD, 2008b).

Internationally, the term NEET has become a statistical indicator used to monitor the labour market and the social situations of young people. Here NEET are defined as young people aged 15–24 years who are neither in employment nor in any education or training (European Commission, 2011). In Europe in 2012, almost 7.7 million young people aged 15–24 were NEET. This was equivalent to 13.2 per cent of the total population of that age, an increase from 12.9 per cent in 2011 (Eurofound, 2014). At this time, the highest levels of NEET were recorded in Bulgaria, Greece, Ireland, Italy and Spain: 18 per cent or more among those aged 15–24. Lower proportions were found in Austria, Denmark, Luxembourg and the Netherlands: below 7 per cent. In the UK, 954,000 people aged 16–24 were NEET in the second quarter of 2014, that is 13.1 per cent of people in this age group (Mirza-Davies, 2014), 55,000 of them aged 16–17.

As with those involved in the criminal justice system and those excluded from school, some groups of young people are disproportionally represented within the NEET group. In the year to March 2013, among 15- to 24-year-olds in New Zealand, 23.2 per cent of Māori and 19.8 per cent of Pacific youth were NEET (MBIE, 2013b). In the UK, young people who have a disability are more likely to be NEET than those who do not (DfE, 2011).

Precursors to being NEET: patterns of vulnerability

Before considering research findings, it must be noted that it is not easy to differentiate between the factors that lead to or cause NEET status and the factors that simply correlate with being NEET (Farrington and Welsh, 2003; 2007).

Research in the UK has consistently identified a range of risk factors and precursors associated with being NEET at age 16–18 (Casson and Kingdon, 2007; Social Exclusion Task Force, 2008; Cusworth *et al.*, 2009). These include:

- Having parents who are poor and unemployed
- Living in a deprived neighbourhood near schools with poor average attainment
- Living in particular circumstances which create barriers to participation:
  - They are or have been in care
  - They become pregnant and a parent in their mid-teenage years
  - They have a disability, SEN or learning disability
  - They are young carers
  - They are homeless
  - They have a mental illness
  - They misuse drugs or alcohol
  - They are involved in offending
  - Pre-16 educational disaffection (truancy and/ or school exclusion)
  - Poor or no qualifications at age 16 plus
  - Dropping out of post-16 educational attainment.

(Coles *et al.*, 2010: 6)

The main precursors for under-16-year-olds of becoming NEET are educational disengagement and educational disadvantage (Coles *et al.*,

2010). Young people who are bullied at school are twice as likely to be NEET at age 16 than their peers (Haywood *et al.*, 2008).

Being NEET at least once before increases the chance of being NEET for six months or more by 7.9 times. This exceeds the likelihood of being NEET for six months or more in relation to pregnancy or parenthood, supervision by the Youth Offending Team, disclosed substance abuse, responsibility as a carer, or fewer than three months post-16 education (Audit Commission, 2010a).

Analysis of the European Values survey (Eurofound, 2012), which considered 15- to 29-year-olds, indicated that intergenerational issues and family backgrounds also impact on the probability of becoming NEET. Having parents who experienced unemployment increased the probability of being NEET by 17 per cent. The children of parents with a low level of education were up to 1.5 times more likely to be NEET than the children of parents who had a secondary education and up to twice as likely as those with parents with a tertiary education. Young people whose parents were divorced were 30 per cent more likely to be NEET.

Young people who are NEET

In the move to more nuanced understandings of those who are NEET, researchers have put forward subcategories of NEET, especially so that policymakers and providers can tailor interventions to support young people more closely to need. Spielhofer *et al.* (2009: 2), focusing on 16- to 17-year-olds, proposed three subcategories of NEET:

- *Open to learning NEET* – about 41 per cent of young people most likely to re-engage in education or training in the short term and tending to have higher levels of attainment and a more positive attitude to school.
- *Sustained NEET* – 38 per cent of young people characterized by their negative experience of school, higher levels of truancy and exclusion and lack of educational attainment.
- *Undecided NEET* – 22 per cent of young people. In some respects similar to the open to learning NEET in their attainment levels, but dissatisfied with available opportunities and their ability to access what they wish to do.

Subsequent research by Allen and colleagues (2012: 1) reframed these groups as:

- *Core or sustained* – young people experiencing longer-term disengagement who were strongly linked to a wider pattern amongst a section of society in terms of poor attainment, experience and expectation that challenges public policy (previously sustained).

- *Floating* or 'at risk' – young people who may be dissatisfied with available opportunities or are most vulnerable to economic downturn and shifting labour markets (previously undecided).
- *Cyclical* or in transition – young people who are likely to re-engage in education, training and the workforce in the short term, tending to have higher attainment and a more positive attitude to exploiting opportunity (previously open to learning).

Other research has posed alternative segmentations. Focusing on 'Learning Status', NIACE (2013) used five categories: 'recent experience of being NEET', 'applied for a course', 'looking for learning opportunities', 'want to learn in future', and 'no plans regarding learning'. These categories reinforce the notion that being NEET doesn't mean one thing, which adds weight to the idea that young people regarded as NEET will need different levels of support and guidance.

Relevant too is consideration of spells of NEET, i.e. the period of time that the young person is NEET. In the UK, the minimum length of a spell is approximately a month (DfE, 2011). Findings from the Youth Cohort Study and Longitudinal Study of Young People in England indicated that 3 per cent of those between the ages of 16 and 19 experienced three or more spells of NEET, 8 per cent experienced two spells, and a quarter were NEET for a single spell (DfE, 2011). Approximately three-quarters of the young people in the New Zealand study had at least one NEET spell lasting for a week or longer: most of these spells were short in duration. Over a quarter of young people had at least one long-term spell – six months or longer – during the six years that they were aged 16–21 (MBIE, 2013a). This group was responsible for approxmately three-quarters of all NEET days experienced when aged 16–21.

Consequences for young people termed NEET

Young people in the NEET category face a loss of individual potential (Coles *et al.*, 2002; Furlong, 2006). Being NEET between ages 16 and 19 is associated with an increased risk of being unemployed five years later (Crawford *et al.*, 2011). Young people who are persistently NEET are more likely to remain unemployed in the longer term. Those in New Zealand who had experienced long-term NEET spells during their teens were less likely to study or train, less likely to be employed, and more likely to have further spells of NEET at ages 20 and 21 than those who had avoided being long-term NEET (MIBE, 2013b).

NEET has consequences for physical and mental health, such as difficult relationships, drug and substance abuse, involvement in criminal activities, and disengagement from life and society (Coles *et al.*, 2002; Eurofound, 2012). Such consequences can impact on families and society as a whole.

NEETs display a higher risk of involvement in risky behaviour, and young NEETs may become engaged in a cumulative set of risk-related behaviours including alcohol and drug abuse and involvement in crime. NEETs involved in crime and substance abuse may end up homeless, which in turn affects employment potential. This spiral may also have longer-term intergenerational outcomes since being unemployed as a parent is likely to impact on the achievements and prospects of the children (Chevalier, 2004; Oreopoulos *et al.*, 2003).

Among 16–18-years-olds categorized as NEET, the following forms of later disadvantage and poor welfare outcomes have been identified:

- Regular bouts of unemployment post-18;
- When in employment, lower job security and lower rates of pay (under-employment);
- Combining the two above – short periods or under-employment with periods of unemployment – in cycles of 'churning' in and out of work;
- Teenage pregnancy and earlier parenting;
- Persistent youth offending resulting in custodial sentences
- Insecure housing and homelessness;
- Mental and physical health problems;
- Use of illicit drugs and transition to the use of class A drugs;
- Earlier death.

(Coles *et al.*, 2010: 7)

Policy responses to NEETs

Policy responses to NEETs, for instance the Europe 2020 initiative Youth on the Move (European Commission, 2010b) and the 2012 Employment Package 'Towards a job-rich economy' (European Commission, 2012), tend to focus on (a) the prevention of young people becoming NEET; (b) labour market policies for young people who are unemployed; and (c) the reintegration/re-engagement of young people who are NEET.

Prevention of young people becoming NEET

Many countries have raised the participation age in an attempt to keep young people in education and training for longer. In New South Wales, Australia, the minimum participation age was raised from 15 to 17 in 2010. Young people were also entitled to undertake approved vocational education and training programmes or training in combination with paid work. In Ontario, Canada, the participation age was raised from 16 to 18 in 2006. Young people could continue their education in school or on an approved learning programme such as an apprenticeship. In raising the participation age, the challenge will be to ensure that young people are offered diverse educational pathways where learner-centred approaches to teaching are paramount and where young people can see the relationship between education and employment (see Chapters 10 and 11).

Other preventative approaches include the early identification of early school leavers (see Chapter 3 for early warning systems), alternative educational provision and more flexible curricula (see Chapter 9), increased career guidance (see Chapter 8), and policies focusing on specific vulnerable geographical areas (Eurofound, 2012).

Labour market policies

Active labour market policies include financial incentives for employers to assist young people in making the transition to the labour market. In England under the Youth Contract a payment of £2,200 is offered to employers and providers who take on 16- and 17-year-olds who are NEET. In Sweden, the general fixed-term employment contract provides similar incentives to employers. In Germany, the Bonus for Apprentice Places provides financial incentives to employers if they take on an apprentice who has low or no qualifications, has intermediate qualifications and has been looking for apprenticeship training for more than a year, who has a learning disability, or who is socially disadvantaged (Eurofound, 2014).

These policies and incentives are unlikely to work for young people who have complex needs and have had long periods of being NEET.

Reintegration of young people regarded as NEET

Although not always explicit in national policies, the research identifying subcategories of NEETs clearly indicates that young people labelled NEET will require different levels of support to enable them to reintegrate into education, training or employment. Young people regarded as open to learning have few barriers to engagement and may require low-level support or none at all. Financial incentives to employers, such as those described in the previous section, may open up opportunities. Those perceived to be undecided do need assistance, but appropriate careers guidance and the development of resilience may help to provide a sense of direction (Audit Commission, 2010a; Gracey and Kelly, 2010). Grist and Cheetham (2011) indicate that this may involve positive experiences, building confidence, and help in connecting to other opportunities. Those regarded as sustained NEET usually have more complex needs and are likely to need high-cost targeted support (Audit Commission, 2010a; Gracey and Kelly, 2010).

Similar to policies aimed at increasing labour market opportunities, financial incentives have been adopted in a number of countries as a means of incentivizing young people to re-engage with education, training and employment. The difference is that these are paid to the young person rather than the employer. Britton *et al.* (2011), evaluated interventions to support NEET and suggested that financial incentives might be the most effective way of incentivizing young people who might otherwise be disengaged.

An example of this approach can be seen in the Activity Agreements piloted in England (2006–2011) and Scotland (2009–2011). Targeted mostly at NEETs aged 16 and 17, Activity Agreements were individually tailored agreements between the young NEET and an advisor: the young person would take part in a programme of learning and activity which would help them become ready for formal learning or employment, and would receive a financial incentive of £30 per week.

The guidance and support afforded by their advisor meant that activities were based on assessment of individual need with a particular aim of breaking down barriers to participation. The young people in both pilots valued the support and guidance received from the advisor, which generally included weekly meetings and a range of activities, including work experience, personal development activities and college-based activities (England: Tanner *et al.*, 2009; Scotland: Stevenson *et al.*, 2011). Although the pilots ceased in England, in Scotland they have been rolled out across all 32 authorities. In England only a minority of participants indicated that payment had been a major motivating factor (Tanner *et al.*, 2009). In Scotland the picture was mixed. Although payment was not raised as the main reason for taking part, it was viewed as a positive aspect of the pilot and for some participants it was crucial (Stevenson *et al.*, 2011). (See Chapter 7 Box 7.5 for an example of how Activity Agreement Pilots provided support to young people with Learning Disabilities and/ or Difficulties.)

Broadly speaking, the Activity Pilots could be regarded as an intervention to support the NEETs within the undecided category, since emphasis was placed on one-to-one advice and guidance and the advisors helped the young people look for jobs, compile CVs, and make college applications. The wider activities enabled the participants to develop self-confidence.

Most countries have initiatives in place to identify and support young people who have left education and training early to help them reintegrate into the system. Typically these focus on the reform of second-chance education systems and include special programmes or schools that enable young people to complete their education and acquire basic competencies (European Commission/EACEA/Eurydice/Cedefop, 2014). Across Europe, but not the UK, one such initiative is second-chance schools. Established in France in the late 1990s, second-chance schools (*école de la 2ème chance* or E2C) are work-based programmes located in deprived areas and organized around the needs of the young adults and their local environment (Arico and Lasselle, 2010). Since its inception, the E2C network has grown and consists of 42 schools operating in more than 110 sites. In some countries, for example Malta and Romania, second-chance education has been targeted at specific groups: in Malta it is young people with a disability, while Romania has targeted rural areas and areas with a large Roma population.

Central to second-chance schools is work-based learning, in the form of internships in local companies, alongside the opportunity to develop basic skills (see Box 6.1).

BOX 6.1 FRANCE SECOND-CHANCE SCHOOL (ÉCOLES DE LA DEUXIÈME CHANCE)

E2C are for adults aged between 18 and 25 years without qualifications who have been out of school for more than a year. Most often these adults had left the school system three years before starting the programme. Registrations can be made at any time in the year. Learners generally spend six and a half months at E2C programmes. They are regarded as trainees and are paid a training wage. The young people learn on the job through internships in companies and through individualized learning modules. Particular features include the use of informal active learning rather than passive learning and the development of partnerships with employers to support the training efforts from the start.

(Cities of Migration, 2014)

While the level of support provided in second-chance schools is more intensive than that offered within the Activity Pilots, it is less than for NEETs with multiple needs, who require more targeted and often psychological approaches such as counselling and mentoring. The illustrations that follow in Boxes 6.2 and 6.3 are targeted at NEETs with complex needs.

Youthreach in Ireland is for 15- to 20-year-olds. They are divided into two priority groups. The first group are school leavers who are unemployed and have no or incomplete qualifications from secondary school. The second target group are those with more complex needs and include lone parents, travellers, referrals from the rehabilitation board, young people released from detention, and those who have appeared before the drug court (Eurofound, 2012). A distinctive feature of this programme is the phased approach taken in enabling young people to re-engage with learning.

BOX 6.2 IRELAND YOUTHREACH

Established in the 1980s, Youthreach is a Department of Education and Skills official education, training and work experience programme for early school leavers aged 15–20. It operates on a full-time, year-round basis and has a continuous intake policy. It offers a programme of general education, vocational training and work experience. Guidance and counselling is an integral part of the programme. The programme can include Further Education and Training Awards Council certification, Junior Certificate programmes and Leaving Certificate Programmes. Students over 16 receive a training allowance. Educational provision is learner-centred and there is substantial one-to-one input.

Programmes have two distinct but sequential stages. In the foundation phase learners are supported in overcoming learning difficulties, developing self-confidence and gaining a range of competencies for further learning. In the progression phase learners are provided with more specific development through a range of educational, training and work experience options.

(Inspectorate Evaluation Studies, 2010)

The YouthBuild programme in the US is for vulnerable young people from low-income families. Many have been in the foster care or juvenile justice system. As with the example from Ireland, the young people receive intensive one-to-one support, and counselling is integral to the programme. What is distinctive is the inclusion of leadership development and civic engagement. The participants share in the governance of their own programme through an elected policy committee, and are actively involved in community affairs. Through this they learn the values and the lifelong commitment needed to be effective and ethical community leaders.

BOX 6.3 YOUTHBUILD US

The YouthBuild programme is for high school dropouts, aged 16–24, from low-income families. It combines community service, vocational training and leadership skills with a graduate equivalent diploma (GED) programme. The young people attend a YouthBuild school full-time on alternate weeks. Classes are small, allowing one-on-one attention. During the other week the young people build housing for homeless and other low-income people where they receive supervision and training in construction skills from qualified instructors. Students take part in a leadership development and civic engagement programme and participate in personal counselling and peer support groups. Currently there are over 270 YouthBuild programmes in 46 states. In 2010, based on data submitted to YouthBuild USA from 131 affiliates, 78 per cent of enrolees completed the programme; 63 per cent of these obtained their GED or diploma; 60 per cent went on to post-secondary education or jobs; 25 per cent enrolled in post-secondary education.

(YouthBuild, 2014)

Endnote

Many young people experience NEET spells as part of the process of making choices about their future, waiting for places at college or university, going travelling or pursuing hobbies. In times of economic recession it is harder to gain employment, particularly if they have left school early with few qualifications. Young people who experience multiple or long-term NEET spells need sustained support to help them return to education and training. This will involve one-to-one support, the development of self-confidence as a prelude to re-engaging with learning, and opportunities for work-based learning. For these young people policy initiatives such as raising the participation age and financial incentives to employers are unlikely to help.

Chapter summary

- Internationally governments are concerned about the NEET population. Evidence suggests that being NEET in the long term will result in poor lifelong opportunities.
- Effective support for those regarded as NEET to return to education, employment, or training necessitates a range of interventions and strategies in accordance with the needs of the young people.
- Some need no intervention, since being NEET is part of the churn between education and employment.
- Some young people need moderate levels of support, including targeted careers guidance and opportunities to develop self-esteem and self-confidence in order to find pathways back to education, training or employment.
- For a minority of young people long-term, more intensive interventions are required. Those found effective include intensive one-to-one support, counselling and guidance, basic skills development, work-based learning opportunities, and teaching that is learner-centred and where participants are respected and valued by those providing the interventions.

Part Three

Issues

Chapter 7

Special educational needs

Overall, young people who have SEN achieve less well than their peers. Compared to their peers, young people with SEN are more likely to truant and be excluded from school. They are far more likely than their peers to be NEET. This chapter considers the barriers they face and how schools, colleges and local authorities can address these.

Context

Young people who have SEN have a wide range of different needs including levels of learning difficulty such as reading and writing, behaviour issues, mental health needs and physical difficulties. Many require support to enable them to remain engaged with education (Audit Commission, 2010b). Internationally, young people with SEN disproportionately come from disadvantaged backgrounds and are more likely to be absent or excluded from school. Overall, they achieve less well than their peers. Once over the age of 16, young people with learning difficulties or disabilities are more likely to be NEET.

Governments worldwide have agreed that all children and young people have the right to education, including those who have SEN. In the Salamanca declaration (UNESCO, 1994) and ensuing legislation from governments since it was signed, the term 'inclusive education' has been adopted, although this has not led to it being used consistently. The characteristics, purpose and form of inclusive education vary depending on national and historical perspectives, social, political, economic and cultural concepts (Mitchell, 2010). Whatever these differences, not all young people with SEN are receiving their entitlement to education. In 2009, UNESCO reported that children with disabilities accounted for one-third of all out-of-school children. Particular challenges include tensions between high-stake assessment demands and the overarching ambition to provide education for all, alongside the recognition of the long-term costs to government when young people with SEN have no employment in later life.

Most young people who have SEN can move into sustained education, employment or training given suitable support and access to work or learning (Audit Commission, 2010b). It is critical that young people with particular needs do not become disengaged from education because the provision offered is inappropriate.

SEN: International perspectives

Definitions of SEN vary across countries although in broad terms a child is recognized as having SEN 'if he or she is not able to benefit from the school education made generally available for children of the same age without additional support or adaptations in the context of studies' (OECD, 2012b: 1). In a minority of countries, for example France, there is no established term which refers to young people who would benefit from specific measures based on their SEN. Definitions vary according to whether children with certain disabilities are included in the category of having SEN. In Greece and Sweden, for example, only children who attend special programmes in special schools or classes are counted, and not those in mainstream schools who have educational needs (OECD, 2012b). National differences also play a part. For instance, there are national and cultural differences among the ways in which social, emotional and behavioural difficulties (SEBD) are defined, and this affects both the presentation and identification of SEBD (Cooper *et al.*, 2013).

A further complication arises because not all are identified as having SEN early in their experience of education. Disabilities are not always apparent until later; educational needs are not reported and are not met. Particularly among young people in alternative provision, their full range of needs may not have been identified: social, emotional and behavioural issues can mask underlying learning needs or disabilities.

Across OECD countries the proportion of children with SEN varies from 1 per cent in Korea to over 10 per cent in the US (OECD, 2012b). In England, the number of pupils who have SEN decreased from 1.55 million pupils (18.7 per cent) in 2013 to 1.49 million pupils (17.9 per cent) in 2014 (DfE, 2014c). This was part of a continuing decline since 2010, when they made up 21.1 per cent of pupils. One possible reason for this decline was the better identification of pupils who do indeed have SEN. This may have been a consequence of the Ofsted (2010c) SEN and disability review, which found that a quarter of young people identified with SEN, and half of those at School Action, did not have SEN. By contrast, in New South Wales, Australia, there has been an increase in the number of young people identified as having one or more disability in regular and in-support classes from 2005 to 2011. This increase was attributed to the increased awareness of disability and of diagnostic characteristics of the students in addition to the boost in funding support for students requiring support (ARACY, 2013).

Some groups of young people are disproportionally represented among those who have SEN. Boys at secondary school in England are nearly three times more likely than girls to have statements of SEN. Pupils with SEN are more than twice as likely to be eligible for free school meals than those without (29.1 per cent compared to 13.4 per cent). Looked-after children are almost four times more likely to have SEN and approximately ten times more likely to have statements than all pupils (DfE, 2014c).

Young people with SEN are also disproportionally represented in the number of students who drop out of school. In the US, data from the academic year 2008–09 indicated that 22 per cent of young people aged 14 to 21 who had disabilities dropped out. Of these, students with emotional disturbance were most likely to drop out (40 per cent), followed by students with specific learning difficulties (21 per cent), other health impairments (20 per cent), and intellectual disabilities (20 per cent) (Snyder and Dillow, 2012, Table 118). Students who have disabilities are more than twice as likely as their peers to receive one or more out-of-school suspensions (US Department of Education, 2012).

Given these challenges, it is perhaps not surprising that young people who have SEN fall behind their mainstream counterparts. In Australia, such students fall behind further in relation to their wealth, education, health and opportunity (ACARA, 2012). In 2012–13, 23.4 per cent of young people in England who had SEN achieved the benchmark of five or more GCSEs at grades A* to C*, including English and Maths, compared to 70.4 per cent among young people without (DfE, 2014d). This pivotal summative assessment impacts on entry to further education and possible courses of study, employment opportunities and career prospects (Demack *et al.*, 2000). Low educational attainment can therefore be a barrier for young people who have SEN accessing work or learning post-16 and lead to unemployment in later life (Audit Commission, 2010b).

Barriers to engagement with education

Ewen and Topping (2012) comment that while the educational experiences of young people identified with SEBD frequently result in exclusion and non-attendance, this is based on the fact that they are characterized by their failure to achieve and their poor conduct within school settings. Issues with low self-esteem and lack of confidence about learning, coupled with difficult background circumstances and emotional difficulties, can form part of an overall picture in which many such young people become disenchanted with the process of schooling.

Research in the UK highlighted the following as barriers to engagement with education for young people who have SEN:

- Lack of suitable provision to meet young people's needs;
- Lack of support during school, or during the transition to post-16 learning or work, leading to disengagement;
- Lack of communication between agencies working with young people, which can result in gaps in support, or failure to join up initiatives;
- Inaccessibility to learning centres or the workplace because of young person's need;
- Stereotyping, or lack of awareness of SEN by employers and educators.

(Audit Commission 2010b: 11)

The location of educational provision

Young people with SEN are educated either in segregated special schools or in segregated special classes in mainstream schools for most of the school day (80 per cent or more), or they may attend regular classes in mainstream schools (OECD, 2012b). Some countries, e.g. Iceland, Ireland, Italy, Norway, Portugal and Spain, include over 75 per cent of young people with SEN in mainstream classes (OECD, 2012b). With the exception of Italy and Poland, all European countries have special classes in mainstream schools. In Denmark and France this is the most common educational setting for the young people who have SEN (OECD, 2012b). In England, about four in ten pupils of primary and secondary school age with statements are in special schools (DfE, 2014c).

In New South Wales, young people access special schools, classes within mainstream schools and funding to support students in regular classrooms (NSW Government, 2012). Within the Australian Capital Territory, students can attend mainstream classrooms, early intervention centres, learning support units and specialist schools. All young people are eligible to access their local school (ACT Education and Training Directorate, 2013).

While not denying the importance of special schools in engaging young people with education, placing them in specialist provision can lead them to develop feelings of exclusion from mainstream society and school (Norwich, 2008). Studies into deaf identity, for instance, found that those educated in special provision for the hearing impaired were likely to form a deaf identity, whereas those attending mainstream provision identified with the social and cultural norms of the hearing community (Nikolaraizi and Hadjikakou, 2006).

Support in schools

The needs of young people who have SEN lie on a continuum. Educational support for young people needs to match individual needs and covers a variety of assistance from additional classroom support to full-time packages of education and specialist therapy (NAO, 2011). In many countries, different forms of support are available to assist the teacher to adapt and modify the curricula and the environment to ensure that they are accessible to learners who have SEN. In New South Wales, support for young people in mainstream schools with a disability includes the school learning support team, the Learning Assistance Program, the Integration Funding Support Program, the School Learning Support Coordinator and the proposed School Learning Support Program (NSW Legislative Council, 2010). Additional, supplementary funding is allocated on a needs-based system. A further range of support services including speech therapy, occupational therapy, physiotherapy and counselling are provided through government and private funders, although there are concerns that provision is inconsistent and rather ad hoc (NSW Legislature Council, 2010).

Ofsted (2010c), in reviewing educational provision for young people with SEN in England, reported that the keys to good outcomes were good teaching and learning, close tracking, rigorous monitoring of progress with interventions quickly put in place, and a thorough evaluation of the impact of additional provision. Where teachers and providers had high aspirations and focused on enabling young people to be as independent as possible, this led most reliably to the best achievement. Among specific interventions to prevent young people with SEN from becoming disengaged from school, the most common are mentoring, interventions targeted to specific disability-related needs, such as alternative provision and vocational training, and class setting and exit options (Wilkins and Huckabee, 2014).

Mentoring

The use of mentoring is a popular intervention worldwide to support students who are at risk of or are already disengaged from education (see Chapter 3). In the Rehabilitation, Empowerment, Natural Supports, Education and Work (RENEW) programme in the US, trained facilitators work with young people with SEBD over a period of 12 months to enable them to develop their plans for their future educational, employment and adult life goals and to coordinate their academic and work-related experiences (Wilkins and Huckabee, 2012). This extensive programme comprises four stages: engagement and personal futures planning, team and plan development, implementation and monitoring, and transition (Malloy, 2013). The futures-planning process is designed to enable each young person to create and then pursue a plan that is based on their individual strengths, needs and preferences. This contrasts with the use of individual educational plans that are often developed without direct input from the student. The long-term relationship with the facilitator is key to enabling the young people to learn how to trust and engage with others and to develop self-efficacy.

On-site separate classrooms

The use of on-site classrooms within mainstream schools for pupils who have SEN is a feature in many countries. Landrum *et al.* (2004) in the US explored dropout among students with emotional and behavioural difficulties to see whether they attended a general education class, a resource room or a separate class. A resource room is a provision for SEN students for less than 60 per cent of the school day, whereas a separate class is attended for more than 60 per cent of the school day. Students receiving education in separate class settings were less likely to drop out than those in general class settings. It appears that for some, on-site provision away from mainstream classes provides a smaller, quieter environment to support their learning. The illustration in Box 7.1 captures the experience of a 13-year-old boy with attention deficit hyperactivity disorder (ADHD) and how attendance at the on-site provision enabled him to manage his behaviour and engage with learning (IOE and NFER, 2014).

BOX 7.1 ON-SITE SEPARATE CLASS PROVISION TO SUPPORT LEARNING
Rob had been at the on-site provision for two and a half months and received tuition for English, maths and science.

> 'In lessons we kept talking and annoying the teachers. I got put on report every day. The school told me that there were two options. I could change schools or go to the on-site provision. I got on well with the teachers when I came here [on-site provision].
>
> It's better here because there's not as many people. My friends are allowed over here on Fridays for break and lunch and I go there for break and lunch sometimes. I prefer it over here.
>
> If I get angry now I can calm down. If that happened in the main school I'd just walk out and slam the door.'

From the teacher's perspective, Rob's behaviour points had dramatically reduced since he was now able to take himself out of the situation.

(IOE and NFER, 2014: 98–9)

The use of flexible timetables coupled with on-site support can work well with young people who have SEN (IOE and NFER, 2014). For instance, one Year 8 boy who had ADHD often struggled in afternoon lessons and was not coping. It was arranged for him to take his work to an in-school support centre for the last lesson in the afternoon. The smaller, more controlled, calmer environment, where teaching assistants were on hand to support him, enabled him to get through the school day.

Transition to secondary school

Young people with SEBD can find transition from primary to secondary school difficult (Osler *et al.*, 2001). Interventions to support young people in the transition from primary to secondary school are discussed in detail in Chapter 8. Here two examples draw attention to the specific needs of young people and the barriers they face.

The specific challenges for young people with Autistic Spectrum Disorder (ASD) include the social and communication demands of the mainstream classroom, the physical setup of the classroom, and the sensory demands of a noisy classroom environment (Humphrey and Lewis, 2008). In Australia, the Autism Spectrum Australia's (Aspect) satellite classes seek to address these issues by providing an environment in which these students can adjust at their own pace, become familiar with mainstream environments and gain skills for managing the mainstream setting. When they transition, teachers from the satellite classes provide support and education for mainstream teachers so they can modify the classroom environment and their teaching style to meet the needs of these students. The satellite classes, for groups of five or six students, are hosted in the mainstream school. Here they receive specialized teaching and have plenty of opportunities to integrate with students in mainstream classes. When a student is perceived to be ready for transition, they undergo a transition process involving meetings, opportunities for mainstream staff to observe them, supported student visits to the main school, and information sharing (Keane *et al.*, 2012).

For students with SEN who are at risk of disengagement it is important that interventions begin prior to transition. The following conditions are required: that effective liaison occurs between the primary and secondary school specialists; that transfer of information and understanding of the students' needs is effective so that support structures are in place from day one in the secondary school; that the transition programme in the secondary school continues to allow time for the student to settle in and where needed, use is made of in-school support centres to support them. Box 7.2 illustrates the value of transition work.

BOX 7.2 TRANSITION WORK TO SUPPORT A STUDENT WITH EMOTIONAL AND BEHAVIOURAL DIFFICULTIES

The primary school perspective

> Mike was identified as 'at-risk' during the transition period as he had emotional and behavioural difficulties and was very withdrawn despite having considerable intellectual capabilities. The primary SENCO [Special Educational Needs Co-ordinator] described him as very needy and indicated that he required support.
>
> Effective liaison work took place with the secondary SENCO, appropriate support was discussed and put in place for Mike from day one of the secondary school and critically he was able to build up a good relationship with the transition worker over a period of time. Without this intervention he would not have attended school, he would have disappeared from the system.

The secondary school perspective

> Mike continues to be isolated in school. He is on the Gifted and Talented list as well as having emotional needs. Family life is very difficult and he gets very little support from his mother. There were major problems with him starting secondary school since he did not have the uniform. Because of the transition worker we found out about this. We managed to get some money to fund his uniform from the LA [local authority]. If it wasn't for this he probably would not have started at all. He is a very big boy and stands out immediately, without a uniform this would have been even worse. He is a very bright lad and is involved in lots of extra-curricular activities. (SENCO)

Mike's perspective

> It's all about moving from primary to secondary school and all the changes. It's about being in a big school and being worried about being bullied. In my primary school I was afraid that I was going to be bullied … I was worried about making friends. I like the lessons and the teachers. I also like the trips. If I hadn't had this support I would have gone off track, I would have been bad. I want to go to college when I finish school and then go to university. Then I want to get a job possibly in a bank. Year 7 has been much better than I thought. I've not been in too much trouble this year, overall my attendance has got better but I did have one slip – I had four weeks off. I've also been excluded once this year and spent the time in the LSU … I don't think I'm going to get excluded next year … I think the transition work was a good thing and that everyone should do it. It made a real difference in terms of my behaviour, having someone to talk to. I haven't really got into any fights this year, I don't get as stressed as much. It's because I've had someone to talk to'.

> (Hallam and Rogers, 2008: 199–200)

SEN and alternative provision

The government's expert adviser on behaviour in the UK, Charlie Taylor, acknowledged that 'the boundaries between alternative provision and SEN provision are blurred' (Taylor, 2012b: 5). In 2011, 79 per cent of students accessing alternative provision through PRUs had a recognized special educational need (Taylor, 2012b). As acknowledged in Chapter 9, alternative educational provision is offered for young people with a broad spectrum of needs.

Alternative provision for those who have SEN can be offered for multiple reasons. These can include: support for transition to progression pathways; the chance for young people who have complex needs to develop independent living skills; the opportunity to test out and experience various activities so they can make informed decisions and choices; and the opportunity to receive intensive support and therapeutic interventions while keeping links with the local community.

Based on a review of interventions for students who had SEN, Wilkins and Huckabee (2014) found that where these young people had the option of taking vocational classes or undertaking alternate school completion requirements, they were more likely to remain in school and complete their studies. In the School Exclusion Trial (IOE and NFER, 2014), the availability of alternative provision was making a difference to the young people who had SEN (see Box 7.3).

BOX 7.3 ALTERNATIVE PROVISION FOR A YOUNG PERSON

One young person, in year 8 was very disruptive in class. He is dyslexic and there was support in place for him but he was always pushing boundaries. We wanted to keep him positive and give him a positive year so we sent him on a six-week agricultural course at the farm where he attends for a day a week. His attendance has massively improved and so has his behaviour. He is also making progress in terms of the curriculum. He'll still be a Level 1 learner, but we're not talking about scraping Gs, we're talking about making Es and pushing him on. He's just had his mock results and they're Es. (Assistant head teacher)

(IOE and NFER, 2014: 100)

In the Back on Track pilots (White *et al.*, 2012), one authority offered education and therapeutic support to 11- to 16–year-olds presenting with behavioural, social and emotional difficulties. They were perceived as hard to place and were struggling in mainstream education. The pilot aimed to support their reintegration into mainstream education, where appropriate, and to prepare others for post-16 transitions. The full-time offer included:

- maths/numeracy, English/literacy, ICT, science, personal social and health education, art, woodwork and cooking, leading towards AQA accreditation since in most cases GCSEs had not been a realistic goal;
- Prince's Trust 'xl' award programme, accredited by ASDAN, where young people undertook structured projects that developed personal and life skills;
- therapeutic services involving counselling, art and massage therapy, family support and therapeutic/positive relationships;
- sports and other activities including visits to leisure centres, the theatre and work experience opportunities.

(White *et al.*, 2012: 17)

Alternative provision for young people who have SEN is effective when it provides a continuum of provision that is delivered in a variety and combination of learning environments that meets their needs and wide-ranging characteristics at an individual level (Martin and White, 2012).

Progression for post-16 learners

Progression post-16 is important for all young people, especially those who may be disengaged from education (see Chapter 8) or who have been involved with the youth justice system (see Chapter 5). For those who have SEN, progression post-16 can be particularly important in order to enable them to develop greater independence, to progress to further study or employment whether supported or open, and/or to provide skills for independent living (Ofsted, 2011a).

FE colleges are the most common destination in England for young people with a statement (54 per cent) and for those who have SEN without a statement (45 per cent) (DfE, 2014c). Ofsted (2011a) reported that too few young people with Learning Difficulties and/or Disabilities (LDD) progressed from school to complete programmes of learning in post-16 settings. At the time, local authorities were required to undertake learning difficulty assessments of all young people with statements of need or in receipt of support before the post-16 transition. The assessments were neither adequately completed, nor done in time and did not form an adequate basis on which to plan or support a programme of study. Placement decisions were unclear, local options were insufficiently considered and work-based learning provision was rarely considered. In addition, the choice of education and training opportunities at 16 was limited for many of the disabled young people and those who had SEN. Few courses were available for those with the lowest levels of attainment (Ofsted, 2011a). The illustration in Box 7.4 provides an example of where a young learner with undiagnosed dyslexia was supported in returning to education.

NEET and SEN

Evidence from the National Audit Office (2012) indicated that nearly one-third of learners aged 16–25 who had LDDs were NEET. In England, an extension to the trial of the Activity Agreement Pilots began in April 2009. This was premised on a new policy model with a specific remit to increase take-up rates among vulnerable young people defined as NEET, including those with LDD. Activity agreements were an individually tailored agreement between the young person and their advisor for a programme of learning and activity that would help them to become ready for formal learning or employment. A specific focus of the agreements were activities that would help them to cope with their LDD. Programmes lasted for 20 weeks, though advisors were aware that this was not long enough to address the barriers that some young people faced. However, the programme could help to equip them with strategies and skills to continue making progress towards an employment or training outcome. One particular finding from the evaluation was that compared to the young people who had participated in earlier Activity Agreement delivery models, these participants had often had very difficult school experiences that had dented their confidence in learning (Maguire *et al.*, 2011). Specific activities to support them are illustrated in Box 7.5.

> ## Box 7.4 Support for a young person with undiagnosed dyslexia
>
> One learner had a poor attendance record at school; she left with no qualifications. She attributed her poor schooling record to undiagnosed dyslexia, and the transition documentation confirmed this. She had found employment in a local garden centre and spent much of her leisure time helping out at local farms, and was particularly interested in working with horses. Her employer recognised her ability and suggested that she consider returning to study.
>
> She attended an open day at a local agriculture college and after discussions with tutors applied for a course leading to horse management. Although she did not have the required qualifications, the college was impressed by her obvious knowledge and understanding at interview. The college identified her dyslexia. Her support plan included opportunities for one-to-one support to help to develop her writing skills.
>
> After three years, she was preparing for a veterinary career, using the college's foundation degree as a first step. She drops in to the open access support centre for help if that is needed, but she has developed strategies to enable her to cope with written work and is now mostly an independent learner.
>
> (Ofsted, 2011a: 30)

> ### Box 7.5 Activity Agreement Pilots: Support offered to young people with LDD
>
> Young people took part in activities that assisted them in coping with their LDD. In addition to specialist support for dyslexia and for moderate learning difficulties, this included strategies to cope with ADHD and impulsive behaviour. Sometimes an activity related to other forms of development, for instance musical skills, but through this young people developed their social skills and increased confidence. Most support was delivered on a one-to-one basis or in small groups. Young people gained or were working towards accreditation in numeracy and literacy. Activities included vocational and employment activities, including activities to develop employability such as CV development and careers advice. Taster activities were offered in beauty therapy, forklift driving, outdoor sports and health and safety training. A central focus was on enabling the young people to develop increased self-confidence and to address barriers that related to their LDD.
>
> (Maguire *et al.*, 2011)

Endnote

Effective educational provision for young people with SEN who are disengaged from education is dependent on the characteristics and ethos of provision, the composition of the educational curricula offer, effective relationships with teachers and providers where they hold high expectations of learners and where joint working and information exchange means that the needs of the young people are understood and met. Having all this in place can make a positive difference to the lives of young people with SEN who are at risk of disengagement or of dropping out of education.

Currently, the quality of educational provision is patchy. Often the curriculum is insufficiently matched to the needs of the young people and, particularly for those over 16, the curriculum offered is limited in terms of the level of qualifications and the vocational opportunities. Communication during transition periods is not always effective or timely, which means that young people with SEN who are at risk of disengagement from education face further barriers because either their needs are not understood or appropriate provision is not in place from day one.

Chapter summary

Young people who have SEN are disadvantaged compared to their mainstream peers and face many challenges if they are to remain engaged in education and training. For educational provision to be effective:

- the needs of the young people have to be assessed in a timely fashion
- the curriculum has to be matched to their needs, interests and aspirations, so they are provided with opportunities for success
- learners are to be held to high expectations
- learners are to be provided with opportunities to develop their self-confidence and self-esteem through a range of activities in addition to the academic offer
- strong, positive relationships with mentors, teachers and providers need to be in place
- transitions need to be supported prior to and after the period of transition
- all the agencies involved need to communicate effectively so that all educational provision is appropriately planned.

Chapter 8

Transitions

Young people negotiate many transitions related to their education, including moving to secondary school or FE and training. For some young people, transitions include returning to mainstream education from attendance at a student support centre, a PRU or alternative educational provision. Young people are faced with decisions at key educational milestones such as the choice of pathways at upper secondary education, when support and guidance is particularly important in ensuring that young people can negotiate transitions successfully. This chapter explores the challenges associated with different transitions for young people who are disengaged or at risk of disengagement with education.

Context

Educational transitions include moving from primary to secondary, Key Stage 3 to Key Stage 4, school to college, and from alternative educational provision to mainstream education. Most young people make successful transitions throughout their education. However, certain groups of young people are more likely to find transitions challenging compared with their peers. Some young people may be particularly vulnerable to school disengagement and adjustment problems during the transition to secondary school. Poor transition experiences are stressful and have been associated with concurrent psychological problems, which can in turn set in motion a chain of events that impact on future attainment (Rice *et al.*, 2010). Dips in attainment occur after key transition points (Galton *et al.*, 2003; West *et al.*, 2010). Where students experience difficulties in making the transition between educational stages, this is associated with lower levels of attainment, less positive attitudes to education and learning, and disengagement from education. Transitioning between educational institutions can make students feel vulnerable and consequently they may become disengaged, with the possibility that they drop out of education altogether. Once students reach their early teens, they are faced with choices to make about the courses they wish to follow. Providing the best possible information, advice and guidance to assist their decisions is important.

Understanding transition

The primary to secondary school transition can affect pupils' emotional and psychological adjustment negatively. This may manifest in behaviours such as poor attendance, lower grades and behavioural problems (Anderson *et al.*, 2000; Smith *et al.*, 2008). Two overarching themes around transition difficulties arise: socio-emotional factors and organizational factors (Evans *et al.*, 2010). Socio-emotional factors include the common anxieties and challenges faced when adjusting to new social and physical environments (Galton *et al.*, 2003; Evangelou *et al.*, 2008). Organizational issues relate to practice within and across institutions, which may ease transition or compound the difficulties (Galton *et al.*, 2003; Evangelou *et al.*, 2008). These relate to the presence or lack of curriculum continuity, collaborative working and sharing practice, and transition support and advice.

Additionally, the transitions that are the focus of this chapter occur during the developmental stage of adolescence: a period of cognitive, psychosocial and emotional transformations (Hines, 2007). As Martinez *et al.* (2011: 526) observe, adolescence is a period of 'significant change and potential turmoil and difficulty', involving multiple factors such as developmental changes and social influence, in addition to school transitions that impact on adolescents' socio-emotional and behavioural functioning. Support from peers, teachers and parents is crucial in shaping teenagers' experiences and outcomes.

Who is at risk during transition?

Transition can be especially difficult for disengaged students, those at risk of exclusion, or with SEBD (Osler *et al.*, 2001), and children and young people from disadvantaged backgrounds (Evans *et al.*, 2010; Martin *et al.*, 2013). Evangelou *et al.* (2008) found that students from a low socio-economic background needed greater help and support to prepare them for the organization and expectations of secondary school. Pupils of low ability are reported to experience more transitional stress and anxiety than their more able peers (Anderson *et al.*, 2000; West *et al.*, 2010). Children with poor socio-emotional skills, low self-esteem or low self-confidence may be vulnerable during transition due to their lack of the skills that would give them the emotional resilience to cope with new expectations and social relationships (West *et al.*, 2010).

Transition is an important time for children to be prevented from becoming missing from education. As Ofsted points out, 'children and young people who are not being educated quickly become at risk of failing academically and socially. If their whereabouts then become unknown, they may be particularly at risk of physical, emotional and psychological harm' (Ofsted, 2010d: 4). Those who are NEET are particularly vulnerable during transition, because of their lack of engagement in schooling (Cowen and Burgess, 2009).

Evidence suggests that young people with the following characteristics may be at increased risk of experiencing difficulties during educational transitions: low socio-economic status, SEN, some ethnic backgrounds, poor record of attendance, low attainment, looked-after and in care and NEET.

Transition to secondary school

The transfer age from primary to secondary school varies from country to country. In the UK, transition is usually at age 11: primary school ends in Year 6 and Year 7 marks the beginning of secondary school. In Australia, students typically transition between age 11 and 13. In New Zealand, many students change schools twice: once between Years 6 and 7, and then again between Years 8 and 9. The age of transition is further complicated in countries such as the US, where children are held back a year if they have not made sufficient progress. Whatever the age when transition from primary to secondary school occurs, it is an important change in the lives of pupils (Galton *et al.*, 1999; 2003; West *et al.*, 2010). It can also be a trigger for school disengagement (Norgate *et al.*, 2013).

Most pupils experience some degree of anxiety about various issues around school transfer (West *et al.*, 2010; Rice *et al.*, 2010). For the majority, these concerns reduce within the first term and the impact of transfer is minimal (Galton *et al.*, 1999), but a significant minority find transition between schools overwhelming (Hodson *et al.*, 2005). The primary to secondary transition may impact on educational attainment (West *et al.*, 2010).

Differences in the structure, complexity and organization of secondary schools compared with those of primary schools include the move from a smaller to a larger school and from having one teacher for most subjects to having different teachers for different subjects, usually in a different room and with different seating arrangements. Young people also encounter new forms of discipline and authority.

Moving to secondary school makes new demands regarding work, such as adapting to a wide range of teaching styles, facing different expectations about homework, and coping with new ways of learning and independent study (Ofsted, 2002). Linked to this is the disjunction between the curriculum in different educational phases and the lack of harmonization of teaching approaches (Galton *et al.*, 1999; Ofsted, 2002).

For the student, social concerns are paramount in their new environment (Mackenzie *et al.*, 2012). As their peer group changes, they worry about social acceptance and this can cause a loss of self-esteem (Frey *et al.*, 2009). Some pupils report being anxious about bullying and afraid of losing their friends (Measor and Woods, 1984). McGee *et al.* (2003), among others, argue that while curriculum continuity is important, insufficient attention has been paid to the social aspects of transition.

A further concern relates to the decline in academic achievement following transition (Galton *et al.*, 1999, 2003; McGee *et al.*, 2003). This dip in attainment occurs regardless of the age of transition, and those who make two transitions experience the transition drop twice (Alspaugh, 1998).

Initiatives have been put in place worldwide to support young people during transition. Some focus on whole-school strategies with a view to improving the transition process for all, whereas others target the young people perceived to be vulnerable. Such has been the increase in transition work that, for example within the UK, a good many pupils who participated in a national survey received some formal support in preparing for the transition to secondary school (Evangelou *et al.*, 2008). While improved transition practices have been shown to be beneficial for all children, those most at risk of difficulties at transition benefit the most (Bryan *et al.*, 2007). The positive transition practice is associated with greater adjustment to the new school environment and improvement in the pupils' social and emotional skills (Evans *et al.*, 2010).

Transition programmes and interventions

Programmes designed to smooth the transition for all pupils include induction days, school visits, information packs, taster days, sharing information between schools and other joint social events between schools (Evans *et al.*, 2010; Evangelou *et al.*, 2008). Other whole-school practices include relaxing the school rules in the first few weeks and helping students to find their way around the school when they start (Evangelou *et al.*, 2008; West *et al.*, 2010). Peer mentoring programmes and buddying systems are popular in the US and arrangements have been made for new pupils to shadow a pupil in their new school for a day so they gain some understanding of what the high school day is like. Schools in New Zealand have used vertical grouping and mixed-ability classes to support pupils with adjusting to secondary school (McGee *et al.*, 2003). Strategies have also included additional pastoral support, buddying with older pupils and mentoring.

As evidenced in Australia and England, some initiatives involve transition teams who visit the main feeder primary schools to explain the secondary school programme, information and open evenings for parents, primary pupils visiting the secondary school to work alongside secondary students in classroom activities, and an orientation day. Transition workers (England) or the school well-being coordinator (Australia) then visit primary schools in September to meet with their teachers and to discuss the students' progress. At Vermont Secondary College, Australia (Vermont Secondary College, 2014), a key part of the approach is Integrated Studies (English, history, and geography), a major part of the Year 7 programme. This enables students to identify with one teacher for a large part of the week as in primary school. Other events to enable students to settle include a Year 7 camp and barbecue held in the first term.

Curriculum interventions (Bryan *et al.*, 2007), such as bridging units in English, science and maths (Galton *et al.*, 2003) and summer schools in literacy and numeracy have been found to help improve young people's attitudes to learning and, in some cases, improve their attainment. Bridging materials in particular can address some of the issues with curriculum continuity: the same work books are used in both Years 6 and 7, and Year 7 teachers visit Year 6 classrooms to watch the class work and talk to individual pupils.

More targeted interventions in the UK include summer schools aimed at pupils from disadvantaged backgrounds (Martin *et al.*, 2013), transition programmes that involve alternative educational provision to support pupils at risk of disengagement, and support from mentors or other staff in non-teaching roles across Years 6 and 7. What is crucial is that pupils perceived as at risk receive support prior to transition (McGee *et al.*, 2003) and longer periods of post-transition support, as they may continue to experience anxieties well into the first year of transition (Ward, 2000).

Across Europe, effective strategies to help young people through transition include the sharing of information between schools, discussions with a mentor or personal adviser, shared projects between primary and secondary schools and joint careers events between schools (Cedefop,

2010). An example of individual support at transition for a pupil with SEN is provided in Chapter 7 Box 7.2.

Reintegration into mainstream education

Young people may be out of mainstream education for extended periods of time for a variety of reasons, including poor attendance, health issues, being at risk of disengagement or due to exclusion. Some may be attending a special school for SEBD and returning to mainstream education. It is vital that strategies are put in place to enable students to reintegrate into mainstream education. For example, one of the concerns about PRUs and alternative educational provision (see Chapter 9) is that they isolate young people from their community and thereby contribute to the negative labelling and stereotyping of those who have additional needs (Norwich, 2008). Similarly, where young people attend in-school support centres (see Chapter 9) support needs to be put in place to facilitate their re-entry into mainstream provision.

Where young people experience attendance difficulties, research indicates that non-attendance rests on a spectrum ranging from occasional reluctance to attend, to complete refusal (Thambirajah *et al.*, 2008). Strategies to support non-attenders back into full-time mainstream education are important before difficulties become entrenched, since the longer young people are out of education, the harder it becomes for them to return. Returning to education may be still harder for those who have dropped out of school altogether. In South Africa, where the incidence of drop-out is relatively high throughout secondary school, the successful reintegration of ex-dropouts is a key priority (Brown, 2013). Young people returning to mainstream education after prolonged absence can find themselves in a difficult position particularly in relation to the amount of work they have missed and have to make up.

The notion that reintegration is important is a near constant message in guidance and policy documents. Speedy reintegration, it is argued, is in the best interest of the young person (Arnold *et al.*, 2009). However, securing successful re-entry to mainstream school is challenging: rates of failure are high, leading to further exclusion or disengagement, especially among older students who have been excluded from school (Parsons and Howlett, 2000; OCC, 2012). In a two-year follow-up study of almost 200 13- to 16-year-olds who had been permanently excluded from schools in England, Daniels and colleagues (2003) reported that only approximately 20 per cent of Year

9 pupils returned from PRU to mainstream school. Some young people are in PRU provision for a long period of time, either because their needs are too great to consider reintegration, as they are awaiting suitable SEN provision, or the schools are unwilling to support reintegration (Panayiotopoulos and Kerfoot, 2007).

Approaches to reintegration need to be timely, individualized and holistic. Some schools use tools to assess the readiness of the young person to return to mainstream education. For instance, the Reintegration Readiness Scale (RRS), subsequently the Coping in Schools Scale, was developed by McSherry (2001) to support children in a special school for emotional and behavioural difficulties transfer into mainstream secondary education. The RSS assesses the students on self-management of behaviour, self-awareness, self-confidence, self-organization, attitude, learning skills and literacy skills, and the students contribute to their assessment. Targets based on areas of weakness identified in the RRS are then set and the student joins a reintegration group that meets on a weekly basis to enable them to set and monitor their own targets in preparation for the move to secondary school. The process of reintegration continues with a key person from the secondary school and the previous school having regular meetings to discuss progress. Parents/carers are involved at every stage of the reintegration.

The focus has recently been on person-centred approaches to reintegration that address issues of power imbalance between the young people and the professional staff. For these to succeed, the students must be actively involved in decision making, the parents must participate and the services must work together. The approach should take account of the observation by Arnold *et al.* (2009) that young people excluded from school are not accustomed to attending meetings in which they are asked for their thoughts and ideas or being listened to by adults in positions of authority. One model is the use of PATH, a person-centred planning tool (Bristow, 2013). PATH places the young person and their family at the centre of the planning process, and utilizes visual strategies to share information.

It is critical that support continues into the mainstream school and that flexible approaches are adopted to reintegration (see Box 8.1). Mainstream schools need to have an inclusive and welcoming ethos, a commitment to responding to and supporting the needs of the young person that include ensuring the involvement of support services and staff to secure successful integration (see Chapter 11).

Box 8.1 Gradual support to reintegration at secondary school

Tina was admitted to the school following difficulties at a previous school, which culminated in her becoming highly disengaged from school and exhibiting a high level of non-attendance. The specialist centre in the school supported a gradual reintroduction to school and education, based on the development of relationships between the pupil, family members and school staff. The following text highlights the parent and head teacher's views of the approach taken.

Tina was having difficulties and wanted a fresh start. She came to the centre and it was about getting her back into education. It was all done at her own pace – getting back slowly into doing her work, and then her uniform. (Parent)

She had been in another school but not attending, I did a home visit and she wouldn't come down the stairs to talk to me – I kept on trying. Eventually she came [into school] for an hour. Next day, she said can she come for two hours? – I said yes. When she was in the centre, there was no educational input – it was all about the emotional support and letting her know what we can do to support her needs. Eventually she built up from half a day to a whole day. (Head teacher)

Then at this point, she asked to go into lessons. Then she surprised us all by going in one day in a full school uniform. She is now on a different course [i.e. direction] and she wouldn't have been able to do it without the support of the school. She's now attending mainstream lessons and doing really well. (Parent)

Tina is now in sixth form and has now moved on to a placement to support her future career. That was arranged through the school. (Head teacher)

(IOE and NFER, 2014: 99–100)

Transitions to further education

Only a small section of examples are given about transition to FE since good practice concerning primary to secondary school transition and reintegration applies equally to young people moving to FE. The atmosphere of an FE college is very different from either primary or secondary school. The teaching methodologies are different and students may need support in developing new study skills. For particularly vulnerable students, for instance those transitioning from PRUs or those regarded as NEET, the move to mainstream FE settings can be unsettling because of the differences in the environment, the personal support received and class sizes (Gracey and Kelly, 2010).

Transitions that are managed well, with focused support, can reduce the risk of learners becoming disengaged, dropping out, and potentially becoming long-term NEET. Effective transitions, similar to transition in schools, require good information sharing, so that as much as possible is known about new vulnerable students and their additional support needs can be met. In some colleges, for instance, the FE 14–19 manager holds case conferences with local schools' Year 11 heads to discuss individual students before they start college (Gracey and Kelly, 2010). Despite areas of good practice, information sharing remains problematic (Ofsted, 2014b).

Young people most at risk of disengagement also need more time to settle into college life. In the evaluation of the School Exclusion Trial (IOE and NFER, 2014), it was evident that strong tracking systems were in place to monitor the destinations of young people after leaving school, alternative provision, or PRU provision. In one local authority where students transitioned from the PRU to the local FE college, the head teacher had realized that the students needed stronger support in making this transition (see Box 8.2).

> ### BOX 8.2 SUPPORT FOR TRANSITION FROM PRU TO COLLEGE
> We track where the pupils go when they leave our provision. This year 89 per cent left with a college or training placement – half a dozen or more are going on to sixth form colleges. Last year retention was far better than in the past.
>
> The same teacher commented on the additional support that was provided to young people to support their transition from the PRU. This included support for interviews, general help with transition and staff going into college with them for the first few days. Where appropriate they also made links with the counsellor at the FE college. This additional support for transition was seen to be having a positive impact on the retention of young people:
>
> > Because in the past we found that too many young people were becoming NEET by November – drop out was too high: 48 per cent retention three years ago, got it up to 78 per cent last year (PRU head teacher).
>
> (IOE and NFER, 2014: 94–5)

Attendance at college pre-16 can help to prepare young people better for the transition to FE at age 16 (Marson-Smith *et al.*, 2009). In line with these findings, some colleges work collaboratively with schools to offer bespoke taster sessions. Other colleges offer taster courses targeted at young people regarded as NEET or who have had little educational success to date. These tasters can give the new students opportunities to try different trades, explore different career paths and get a sense of what they might be interested in studying (see Box 8.3).

BOX 8.3 TASTER COURSE

Croydon College in South West London offers a Fresh Start Programme for 16- to 18-year-olds who have had limited success in education to date. The 12-week programme runs every term and offers vocational tasters in hair and beauty, health and social care, retail, construction, motor vehicle and art and design. In addition it provides functional skills development in English and maths.

(Ofsted, 2014b: 15)

Information, advice and guidance at educational milestones

As young people move through secondary school, they can become demotivated and uninterested in education because they find the curriculum irrelevant to their needs (see Chapter 10). Some drop out of school in response to the traditional style of academic teaching. The challenge then is twofold. First, the school needs to offer attractive and relevant educational pathways to encourage students to stay in school or training and gain an upper secondary qualification (OECD, 2012a). Second, it is critical to ensure that young people receive appropriate guidance about the different pathways available to them and that they make informed decisions about their course of study. Curriculum issues are discussed in Chapter 10. The focus here is on the information, advice and guidance (IAG) required.

Strengthening IAG is a core strategy for helping to improve education transitions. Important is the availability of impartial, accessible and personalized advice, so that young people make the right choices and are well supported during transitions (Evans *et al.*, 2010). High-quality IAG can lessen the risk of students' dissatisfaction with their choice and thereby reduce the likelihood of them dropping out (McCrone and Filmer-Sankey, 2012). The converse is true: poor IAG can result in young people embarking on post-16 courses that do not suit their needs or aptitudes (Ofsted 2013).

For those making the transition to FE and work-based learning, evidence suggests that one main reason for leaving early was that the course was not what they had expected (Simm *et al.*, 2007). Timely and appropriate guidance helps young people develop positive attitudes to learning and to find education, training or employment opportunities.

Young people in different countries are required to make educational decisions at different ages. In Denmark, lower secondary education finishes at age 15 and students choose either an academically oriented upper secondary school programme, or VET. In the Netherlands, children (or their parents) first choose an education pathway at age 12. At age 14, those on a vocational pathway choose between four areas of study, and then at 16 they set out on different levels of qualifications. In France, decisions are made at the age of 14. In the UK, young people make educational decisions at ages 14 and 16, and the options taken can enhance or constrain their life chances (Haynes *et al.*, 2013).

Although good IAG provision is in place in the UK, not all young people receive it (Ofsted, 2013). For example, in schools with weak sixth forms, students have been encouraged to continue on academic courses that they then abandon, in some cases leaving with no additional qualification at all. The approach taken to IAG relates to the characteristics of individual schools. Schools with a student-centred approach (see Chapter 11) and without sixth forms seem to operate on the basis of the needs of their students and work with external agencies to provide IAG. By contrast, schools with sixth forms, and where the institution and its image are most important, have minimal connection with external careers advisers and focus their IAG on progression into their own sixth forms (Hughes and Gration, 2009; Ofsted, 2013). Schools that lack high levels of employer engagement leave their students unaware of the employment opportunities in their local area (Ofsted, 2013).

UK schools provide more IAG for certain young people, including those who have SEN, learning difficulties or disabilities, and potential NEET. Generally, however, IAG offers more one-to-one interviews rather than individualized approaches (McCrone and Filmer-Sankey, 2012). In Victoria, Australia, under the Managed Individual Pathways initiative for all young people aged 15 and over, young people at risk of disengaging or failing to make a successful transition to FE, training or secure employment are provided with targeted support, including access to Student Welfare Coordinators, Student Support Service Officers, community-based agencies and programmes of mentoring and workplace learning (Sweet *et al.*, 2010).

Although not specifically targeted at students at risk of disengagement, an interesting whole-school approach to providing IAG is featured in Box 8.4. This US model offers a long-term approach to IAG that supports young people to progress to FE or employment and which appears to be beneficial to all students, including those at risk of disengagement. It is an antidote to IAG that is often not provided early enough, and to the fact that young people often leave courses because they were not what they had expected and those offering IAG do not know enough about local employment opportunities. In the US case study, students were able to see the relationship between their academic work and how it related to employment. They were presented with a rich variety of experiences during the programme, engaged in meaningful hands-on activities and were given the ability to explore multiple pathways in preparation for the transition to college or work.

> **BOX 8.4 US CAREER ACADEMIES**
> Established over 40 years ago in the US, career academies are small, career-themed schools. Students attending career academies come from a wide range of socio-economic and racial/ethnic backgrounds, with different academic achievement levels and different educational and career aspirations. Students take classes together as a cohort for three or four years, remain with the same group teacher over time and spend time in local work sites to experience the world of work. The curriculum includes both college preparatory courses and a sequence of career-technical courses. Teachers of core subjects and teachers of career-technical courses collaborate in an effort to integrate their content and to emphasize the relevance of what they are teaching to their students' future careers. Students participate in work-based learning activities, such as summer internships, to reinforce those connections and to afford them the opportunity to learn skills for success both in the workplace and in post-secondary education.
>
> (Visher *et al.*, 2013)

Endnote

Transitions are challenging, especially for young people at risk of becoming disengaged from education. Well-managed transitions, where good information sharing takes place, where interventions begin prior to and continue after transition, and where young people are fully involved in the transition process, can help young people to remain in education. While evidence of good practice exists, provision is variable and does not always offer adequate support to young people. Insufficient use is made of tracking systems to monitor the destinations of young people disengaged from education when they move from alternative provision or school. Where the students are making decisions about subject choices as part of their transition, IAG can play an important role in improving their transitions. Too often evidence suggests that young people who are disengaged from education are given little guidance about different pathways and embark on courses that do not suit their needs or aspirations.

Chapter summary

- Effective approaches to transition involve good liaison between the receiving institution and the current school or college. Students disengaged from education need and deserve support mechanisms to be in place from day one in their new environment. Transition programmes need to begin prior to transition and continue after the transition to enable young people to settle in.
- For reintegration to be successful, all the above apply. However, some young people may need longer to adjust to their new environment and institutions would benefit from adopting staged approaches when required.
- Effective IAG for young people at risk of disengagement is based on collaborative and personalized approaches, appropriate timing with appropriate programmes of support put in place and strong links with employers. The staff of some schools need to increase their engagement with employers so that they are aware of opportunities in the locality.

Chapter 9

Alternative educational provision

This chapter explores how alternative educational provision can help to re-engage disengaged young people with education. Consideration is given to the nature of alternative curricula internationally, the characteristics of young people attending alternative provision, the quality of alternative provision, and the characteristics of effective provision. Two extended case studies are provided that exemplify good practice, in order to gain an in-depth understanding of factors that contribute to successful alternative provision.

Context

Most alternative curricula in the developed world were implemented in secondary education in an attempt to encourage young people to remain in school and re-engage with their learning. Evidence shows links between disengagement and an overly prescriptive curriculum that lacks relevance. Alternative curricula in the developed world are many and varied, ranging in a continuum from informal work experiences through to formalized curricula. Variation is also seen in the reasons why children and young people may be placed in alternative education, since internationally alternative provision caters for students who are at risk of exclusion, who have been excluded or suspended, who are unable to thrive in a mainstream environment, or who have medical issues. Young people may be engaged in alternative provision on a full or part-time basis, be it for a time-limited short-term intervention over some weeks or for a longer period. Alternative provision operates in different locations. Some provision takes place in mainstream schools, while on other occasions young people are educated at different sites such as youth centres, farms or FE colleges. Providers of alternative education include public, private and third sector organizations. Evidence suggests that many young people, especially those aged 15 or 16, will remain in alternative provision until the end of compulsory schooling.

The nature of alternative curricula

Many schools, educational authorities, private and third sector organizations throughout the world have developed alternative programmes in order to devise educational provision that better meets the needs of at-risk students whose circumstances make the traditional school setting unsuited to their needs. Terminology varies across countries, be it alternative educational provision, alternative curricula, alternative learning, re-engagement programmes or flexible learning programmes. A key policy focus relates to the belief that supporting young people's education through alternative provision can make a long-term contribution to society in addition to the life chances of those receiving it.

Providing effective alternative curricula is complex, since the young people in this provision have a diverse range of needs. Alternative provision needs to be capable of providing support to students who face various barriers to learning and engagement with education. In England, alternative provision is arranged by local authorities for pupils who, because of exclusion, illness or other reasons would not otherwise receive suitable education. Alternative provision is arranged by schools for pupils on a fixed period exclusion. Schools also have the authority to direct pupils to off-site alternative curricula provision to improve their behaviour (DfE, 2013).

Young people in England attend alternative curricula for a range of reasons: as part of a continuum of support for challenging or vulnerable students, to counter disengagement that takes the form of poor attendance or behaviour, to extend the types of experiences and styles of learning offered, to minimize the impact of some students on the majority, or as a last resort when students are in danger of permanent exclusion (Ofsted, 2011b: 11–12).

Many developed countries offer alternative provision for those who are regarded as at risk of disengagement or who have already disengaged, and separate provision is often in place for those who have been excluded or suspended from school for varying lengths of time. For instance, in Queensland, Australia, three different types of alternative provision are offered: positive learning centres, district-based centres and flexible learning services. Positive learning centres provide alternative education for students who need intervention beyond the capacity of the mainstream classroom. The aim is to reintegrate students into mainstream schooling or into more appropriate learning or vocational pathways. District-based centres provide alternative programmes for students at risk and for young people with 6 to

20-day suspensions. Flexible learning services focus on programmes to re-engage disengaged 15- to 17-year-olds.

In Norway, alternative schools are for pupils who cannot adjust to the demands and expectations of mainstream school life (Harper *et al.*, 2011). In New Zealand there are 14 activity centres, which provide alternative education for secondary students, most of whom are in Years 9 and 10. Generally students are referred because their behaviour impedes their learning or that of others (ERO, 2013). Many students attending activity centres have long histories of disengagement in school. Alternative schools and programmes in the US are designed to meet the needs of students that usually cannot be met in regular schools (Carver and Lewis, 2010). Alternative schools are generally housed in a separate facility where students are removed from regular schools, in contrast to alternative programmes, which are housed in mainstream schools.

Provision for alternative curricula in England includes PRUs, hospital teaching services, home tuition services, virtual or e-learning centres, FE colleges, training providers, employers, voluntary sector organizations, community services, youth services, youth offending teams and other local agencies (QCA, 2004). The type of provision ranges from therapeutic independent schools for children with severe behavioural, emotional and social difficulties to a local provider offering training, say, in car maintenance for one or two pupils (Taylor, 2012b). Alternative curricula include vocational and work-related activities, personal and social learning, as well as more academically focused content (Martin and White, 2012).

In Canada, alternative provision is based on a four-stage continuum of approaches to re-engage students in education:

1. Prevention – strategies such as positive school atmosphere, a range of pathways in school, and transition plans for new or returning students.
2. In-class and in-school interventions – measures such as special education support, transferring to another school, tutoring, coaching, community agency support and credit recovery.
3. School board interventions such as alternative education programmes.
4. Supervised Alternative Learning where 14- to 17-year-olds are excused from school and continue their learning under the supervision of the school board.

(Ontario Ministry of Education, 2010: 8–9)

This is similar to the approach developed in Victoria, Australia (DEECD, 2010). Few developed countries appear to have no system of alternative provision, but the Netherlands and Sweden do not (Harper *et al.*, 2011).

Characteristics of young people attending alternative curricula

Young people referred to PRUs and alternative provision come from the most deprived backgrounds, often from chaotic homes in which problems such as drinking, drug-taking, mental health issues, domestic violence and family breakdown are common. These children are often stuck in complex patterns of negative, self-destructive behaviour and helping them is not easy. Many have developed mental health issues. Breaking down destructive patterns requires the time, effort, commitment and the expertise of dedicated professionals working in well-organized, well-resourced and responsive systems (Taylor, 2012b). Working in alternative provision is clearly challenging.

In England, students accessing alternative provision include:

- those permanently excluded from school or in danger of exclusion
- those with persistent absence from school including anxious school refusers
- those with long gaps in education
- young people with SEN – diagnosed or not; SEN statement or not
- those receiving education other than at school
- new arrivals without a school place
- those with complex social and emotional needs
- young people from disadvantaged or challenging backgrounds
- young carers
- teenage parents and pregnant teenagers
- those with health problems, especially mental health
- alcohol or drug users
- looked-after children
- young people at risk of, or engaging in offending behaviours.

(White *et al.*, 2012: 9)

Young people in the US who attend alternative schools or programmes are typically at risk of educational failure, as indicated by poor grades, truancy, disruptive behaviour, pregnancy, or similar factors associated with temporary or permanent withdrawal from school (Carver and Lewis, 2010).

The proportion of those in alternative provision varies between countries. In New Zealand, alternative education students include more boys, more students aged 14 and 15, more Māori and Pacific, and more from neighbourhoods of high socio-economic deprivation (Clark *et al.*, 2010). Such students are more likely than mainstream students to live under conditions of socio-economic deprivation and stress (Clark *et al.*, 2010). In the UK, boys are more likely to be excluded from school and consequently dominate alternative provision (Russell and Thomson, 2011).

Concerns about the quality of alternative curricula

Too much alternative provision internationally does not meet the needs of young people effectively. Often the curriculum lacks challenge and the qualifications on offer are viewed as marginal by society (Thomson and Pennacchia, 2014). It is suggested that some teachers privilege aspects of well-being in students at the expense of a curriculum offer, thus adjusting educational expectations (te Riele, 2014).

The evaluation of the Back on Track pilots for alternative provision indicated that some young people made behavioural improvements, increased attendance, developed their social, emotional and health well-being, and improved their learning experiences and outcomes (White *et al.*, 2012). However, attainment for students in alternative provision is generally low and is not commensurate with their peers in mainstream education. In England in 2012–13, only 1.5 per cent of such students achieved five or more A* to C grades in their GCSE, including English and Maths, as compared to the national average in England of 59.2 per cent (DfE, 2014d).

The Ofsted survey of alternative provision (2011b) drew attention to specific weaknesses within alternative curricula. Some students were taught in poor quality accommodation. Schools and units were ill-informed about the need for providers to register with the Department for Education (DfE) if they were providing full-time education. Clearly defined success criteria were generally lacking at the outset and monitoring was weak. The process of finding and commissioning alternative provision varied widely. While the majority of alternative provision placements offered some form of accreditation, most was offered at Entry Level or Level 1. The information given to the alternative provider about the students prior to the placement was not always adequate, particularly in relation to SEN, literacy and numeracy. The Taylor review (2012b) confirmed the issues highlighted in the Ofsted survey and identified the following areas for improvement: the planning of individual placements to meet pupils' needs more specifically, the assessment of pupils' needs, the expectations of academic attainment in

English and maths on the part of commissioners and providers, information sharing between commissioners and providers, quality assurance of provision, and collaboration between commissioners, providers and other relevant services.

This concern about the effectiveness of alternative provision led to a raft of measures being put in place to address these issues, including the opportunity for setting up alternative provision academies and free schools and an increasing focus in Ofsted inspections on the behaviour, attainment and safety of students in alternative provision. However, a follow-up report by Ofsted (2014c) demonstrated that while improvements had been made, serious concerns remained. Some students missed out on English and maths teaching, insufficient schools were evaluating the impact of alternative provision on the outcomes for the students, the reporting of students' progress by the provider to the school was often weak, on occasion the accommodation at the alternative providers was unsuitable, not all schools were ensuring that students attending alternative provision received a full-time education, and schools were occasionally using providers that should be registered as independent schools or PRUs, but were not (Ofsted, 2014c: 5).

Further issues relate to the working conditions of teachers in alternative provision as seen in the UK and Australia. Evidence suggests that teachers work long hours, often for lower pay than their counterparts in mainstream education, and have less job security (te Riele, 2014). They may feel isolated and disconnected from their peers and find it difficult to access opportunities for professional development and supervision (KPMG, 2009). These issues may act as a disincentive for staff to continue working with disengaged students and might be a deterrent to potential new staff members.

Good practice in developing alternative educational provision

Internationally, the evidence suggests that effective alternative provision can make a positive difference to young people (Mills and McGregor, 2010; Clark *et al.*, 2010). Within the UK, good alternative provision is defined as that which appropriately meets the needs of pupils and enables them to achieve good educational attainment on a par with their mainstream peers (DfE, 2013). Although alternative provision is highly diverse and there is no single delivery model, purpose or beneficiary group (Gutherson *et al.*, 2011), common characteristics are shared internationally. Alternative curricula provision is usually small in size. Emphasis is placed on developing strong supportive relationships between students and teachers, but with teachers setting clear boundaries and structures. All students are afforded opportunities for success relating to their future, whether the immediate context is education or employment. Teachers have high expectations of their students. An individualized approach is adopted to developing bespoke provision for students that takes into account an assessment of student needs and affords students some control over their learning. Students are offered engaging and meaningful curricula, which often make use of vocational or hands-on learning, and there is flexibility in the nature of provision (see Gutherson *et al.*, 2011; Hallam *et al.*, 2010; Harper *et al.*, 2011; KPMG, 2009; Martin and White, 2012; Mills and McGregor, 2010; te Riele, 2014; Thomson and Pennacchia, 2014; White *et al.*, 2012).

For those responsible for commissioning it, effective alternative provision is characterized by strong quality assurance mechanisms in relation to referral, commissioning, and progression and by continued attention paid to the tracking of student re-engagement with education and academic attainment (IOE and NFER, 2014; Martin and White, 2012; White *et al.*, 2012).

The extended illustrations that follow exemplify good practice for young people in alternative provision.

SkillForce

SkillForce is an education charity working with 10,000 young people in schools in Great Britain who are in danger of leaving school without the skills and qualifications they need to succeed in life. Over the last ten years, SkillForce has delivered qualifications and positive outcomes to over 35,000 young people, with consistently outstanding results. SkillForce Instructors are mainly ex-services personnel with diverse life experiences who provide positive role models for the disengaged participants. The vision of SkillForce is that every young person, whatever their background or ability, is given the chance to fulfil their potential and become a valued member of their community. In partnership with schools, SkillForce delivers a curriculum and activities that provide knowledge, skills, experience, long term personal support and the self-belief to aspire and achieve.

The SkillForce Zero Exclusions pilot took place during 2011–13 and comprised a series of initiatives that were implemented with different groups of young people in England. The aim was to enable secondary students at risk of disengagement to re-engage in education and to enable young people to achieve their full potential. Pupils were in Key Stage 3 or 4 and attended the programme either full or part-time depending on the delivery model in their locality. Activities took place either in a separate building in the main school site or off-site. Among the factors contributing to the success of the programme were the following: a careful induction process; effective use of boundaries, rules, consequences and rewards; strong relationships between participants and SkillForce staff; engaging and meaningful curricula; opportunities for success for all participants; and a strong desire by the SkillForce staff to raise aspirations among their charges (Hallam *et al.*, 2012; 2013).

Pivotal to success were the strong relationships that developed between the participants and the SkillForce staff. It was this that enabled effective learning. SkillForce staff acted as role models, treated young people as adults, listened to their problems and supported them in developing a positive life path (see Box 9.1 and Chapter 11).

BOX 9.1 A PARENT'S PERSPECTIVE OF SKILLFORCE: STRONG RELATIONSHIPS WITH STAFF AND CONTINUED SUPPORT

'He wasn't getting on in school. The school offered that he can go there and he's been there ever since. I wasn't sure what it was going to give him, I didn't have any expectations. I'm very happy with the way it's gone because he has matured a lot. He's been at school. He has kept himself there and he is sitting his exams. I'm over the moon, I couldn't ask for any more. He is definitely better. There is not a big group of them like in school and he probably gets one-to-one and a bit more time given with them. He has calmed down a lot. His attendance is great. It's getting better since SkillForce because he was truanting and not turning up in mainstream school. He is sitting his exams, he has done a few of them now. I don't think it would have gone that far if it hadn't had been for SkillForce, he would have landed with absolutely nothing. He has matured, he's been a better person coming from SkillForce.

They have got a placement in the college for him and at the moment he wants to go into apprenticeship. He really wants to take things on board. Maybe it was a bit easier on one-to-one rather than in the classroom. Having the same teacher every day, not going from one to another made it easier. I think they are just great, I couldn't ask them for any more than what they have done. They've done really well with him, I'm really happy.' (Mother)

(Hallam *et al.*, 2013)

The students engaged in a wide range of activities. All programmes included a variety of out-of-school activities, e.g. rock climbing, improving the environment of the local community, country walks, tracking, orienteering, laser quest, visits to historical buildings, visits to the local fire brigade, visits to the local elderly people's home, painting and decorating outdoor furniture, a variety of sports, plastering, in addition to written work reporting on the activities. More classroom-based activities included designing balloon cars, games, cooking, making knots, and lessons on first aid and substance misuse.

According to the parents, it was the active nature of the activities that made a difference to the young people:

> It was a better opportunity for him. He was more involved while at the minute he lacks concentration at school. When he was with them he was involved in doing something as a team, he was more interactive and getting on and doing things. (Parent)
>
> (Hallam *et al.*, 2013)

The school staff noted that SkillForce staff helped students to realize their career aspirations:

> These students often have poor aspirations and SkillForce show them new opportunities. The staff participate in students' meetings with various employers and can then talk to students about it in a relaxed, trustworthy way which can't be done by unfamiliar career advisors. They are able to guide and support them in aspirations that are appropriate to their needs.
>
> (Hallam *et al.*, 2013)

Participating in SkillForce had supported some of the young people in developing a clear career path (see Box 9.2).

BOX 9.2 SUPPORT WITH PROGRESSION

'He got chucked out of school. I'm quite surprised how well he's done. I don't know yet until he has his results, but the teacher says that he could get five GCSEs. He is much better, he's not as cheeky now and he seems to have grown up. He was not bad at attendance. He knows what he wants to do. He wants to be a mechanic so they are getting him to do the college. He has got more confidence. He has always wanted to be a mechanic. He wanted to have a job. Now he knows that he has to have a qualification before he can do that.

They were on the phone once a week telling us how he was doing. They kept us informed all the time. They are brilliant.' (Parent)

(Hallam *et al.*, 2013)

The School Exclusion Trial

The School Exclusion Trial (SET) (IOE and NFER, 2014) tested the benefits of schools having greater responsibility for meeting the needs of permanently excluded pupils and those at risk of permanent exclusion. This included schools having more responsibility for commissioning alternative provision, and local authorities passing on funding to schools for this purpose. The trial started in autumn 2011 and ran until August 2014. It involved volunteer schools drawn from 11 local authorities in England.

Comparison and trial schools used a range of different providers and types of alternative provision for pupils excluded from school. Specialist support, for instance, Child and Adolescent Mental Health Services, and PRUs were the most common type of alternative provision, followed by individual work placements, time spent in another school, additional services offered by the local authority (such as Traveller education support services or a looked-after children team), and time spent in an FE college.

It was critical that provision matched the needs of the young people. Many local authorities had detailed procedures in place to enable this to happen (see Box 9.3).

> **BOX 9.3 IMPROVED USE OF DATA BY A PRU TO ENHANCE THE COMMISSIONING AND REFERRAL PROCESS**
>
> Information-gathering exercises, involving all relevant stakeholders, underpinned the referral process and focused on the Common Assessment Framework (CAF) and Team around the Child (TAC) meetings.
>
> When school staff wished to refer a pupil to the PRU they were required to initiate a TAC meeting attended by a senior staff member of the PRU. The PRU then requested data on the pupil's prior attainment and background information on behaviour, existing interventions and other support needs. PRU staff conducted a home visit and held an admissions meeting. Due to this, the assessment process was well underway before the pupil entered the PRU. Once the PRU had agreed to accept the referral, the school then commissioned the place, based on the conditions of a standing collective agreement between local schools to fund the PRU to deliver alternative provision and support on their behalf. Further assessments then took place, including academic assessment, to determine the pupil's situation and to establish the portfolio of provision to be put in place.
>
> (IOE and NFER, 2014: 51)

Schools in the trial local authorities made effective use of data to identify patterns of behaviour so they could provide appropriate support packages for young people. Local authority leads and lead teachers in trial schools commented that partnership working had increased and processes had been made more rigorous; that they had better information about pupils and better tracking processes.

Continual monitoring and assessment were an important part of the ongoing quality assurance of external alternative providers. These ongoing systems ensured that the progress the students made was monitored and action taken if they needed more support (see Box 9.4). In many instances the local authority retained a quality assurance role and had a list of alternative providers who were registered and approved by the authority, which conducted lesson observations.

Box 9.4 Monitoring, assessment and quality assurance of external providers

Prior to commissioning, quality checks were undertaken in relation to health and safety, child protection and insurance documents. All providers wishing to be commissioned were required to be certified by a relevant awarding body. Once PRU staff were satisfied that prerequisite policies and standards were in place, a generic service level agreement was established. This set out details of the 'client group', the 'types of pupils they worked with', the contract price and what the cost of the provision covered, for example, personal protection equipment, lunches and transport. The agreement also covered the level and nature of the provision to be offered and the expected pupil outcomes.

Following the commissioning of a provider, the head of the PRU and the curriculum manager conducted six-monthly reviews of all providers to ensure that previously agreed performance targets had been met and to negotiate future targets.

Providers were required to complete a pro-forma on a weekly basis that included details of pupils' attainment and attendance. Senior members of the PRU staff reviewed these documents. These weekly reports supported the PRU's operation of a traffic light system for monitoring pupils' progress, leading to the instigation of the LA [local authority]-wide graduated response system to behaviour and attainment, if this was seen to be necessary.

(IOE and NFER, 2014: 58–9)

Partnership working increased throughout the trial. Lead teachers commented that the strengths of their alternative provision arrangements depended on collaboration and good relationships with the local authority, other schools and providers. Box 9.5 demonstrates how this enhanced level of collaboration enabled a number of disengaged young people to benefit from vocational provision.

Box 9.5 COLLABORATIVE USE OF VOCATIONAL FACILITIES

One school providing in-house AP [alternative provision] also acted as an AP provider to other schools. The school had on-site vocational AP including car mechanics, beauty and construction. The size of the provision was fairly small: the garage took 16 pupils, construction 14 pupils and beauty 11. This limited the offer but qualifications were being offered at Level 2. The school itself used the provision for two days per week, whilst two days were allocated to AP for other schools and the final day was allocated to former PRU pupils.

The school marketed itself as a provider of vocational provision and was in the approved provider catalogue for the local authority. Being both a vocational and mainstream provider meant that pupils felt that they were part of the community:

> 'We're in a different position because we are a vocational provider as well as a mainstream school and we understand these types of young people that are coming in. The young people don't see our alternative provision as a bolt-on, they see themselves as still part of the community and don't see it as 'you just want to get rid of me'. (Head teacher)
>
> (IOE and NFER, 2014: 59)

Endnote

Alternative educational provision can make a positive difference to young people. Despite evidence that alternative provision is improving, specific challenges remain to all those working in this context. Young people are not always sufficiently enabled to achieve their best because of continued offers of low-level qualifications that are often unattractive to employers. Not enough attention has been given to alternative provision for 16- to 18-year-olds. It is likely that this will be exacerbated as governments raise the participation age. Just as the needs of older students are not being met, there are issues with the nature and scope of alternative provision for girls because of the over-representation of boys. The tracking of young people when they have left alternative provision remains problematic, yet more needs to be known and understood about the pathways young people take. Providers of alternative provision need more robust approaches to evaluating the outcomes for young people so they can demonstrate success. Teachers working in alternative provision require high-level skills and more needs to be done to ensure that their experience is valued.

Chapter summary

Common factors that contribute to the success of alternative provision include:

- a curriculum matched to the needs of the individuals so they can demonstrate success and pathways to further learning and training
- strong, trusting relationships with their teachers, ideally in a small group setting
- effective assessment of the needs of young people, which is to be communicated to all those working with them, especially during the transition to alternative provision
- opportunities to engage in practical and vocational work that relates to the students' aspirations.

It is essential that those commissioning alternative provision secure the following:

- strong quality assurance mechanisms applied to referral, commissioning and progression
- continued attention to student re-engagement with education and academic attainment.

Chapter 10

Curricula and pedagogy

> One of the main factors associated with disengagement and drop-out is the mismatch between the curriculum and the interests and aspirations of students. Young people who are disengaged from education often fail to see the relevance of the curriculum to their current or long-term interests. Throughout the book there are examples of innovative provision for disengaged students. This chapter explores how different pedagogic approaches and a wider curricula offer can re-engage young people with education. Examples describe a more personalized curriculum, the value of informal learning, embedded approaches to English and maths, and the use of technology to engage learners.

Context

The curriculum offered in schools, colleges, YOIs, alternative provision, and other educational institutions is important in engaging young people in education. Many, as we have seen, find the curriculum irrelevant to their needs, unrelated to the workplace, unappealing in the manner in which it is delivered and boring. A specific issue lies in the mismatch between the academic curriculum offered and the interests and skills of the students (Callanan *et al.*, 2009; Hartas, 2011; Lloyd Jones *et al.*, 2010). Research undertaken in Malta (MT, 2012) suggests that the lack of relevance explains why so many leave education before they gain qualifications. Additional concerns relate to the formality and prescription of the curriculum and inherent difficulties with the emphasis on a literacy-based curriculum (Hilton, 2006). Allied to this is the perception that the curriculum has become increasingly academically oriented (Hartas, 2011). Some countries require low-achieving students to repeat a grade, which adds to disengagement. The frequent testing of young people throughout their education also has a negative impact (Hayward *et al.*, 2009).

Ways have been found to enhance the educational offer, such as wider, richer curricula with better vocational provision, increased flexibility of provision, and greater relevance. Pedagogic practice needs to engage the student, so must be designed from an understanding of their requirements. This means acknowledging the young people's interests and building on their prior knowledge and skills (Davies *et al.*, 2011). Effective educational programmes make increased use of collaborative work, involve the students in deciding about learning activities and the construction of their learning, adopt applied or hands-on approaches to learning, address literacy and numeracy needs in authentic contexts, and use digital technologies to re-engage students with education.

A wider, more personalized curriculum offer

It is important that students be given the opportunity to have choice in the curriculum and qualifications they study (Gracey and Kelly, 2010). Personalized approaches, having high expectations, flexibility and positive relationships built on mutual respect and trust are effective with vulnerable young people including those in alternative provision, those with learning difficulties, or members of ethnic minority groups, such as Gypsy, Roma, and Traveller pupils (Wilkin *et al.*, 2009; Kendall *et al.*, 2007). Ofsted (2010a: 20) concluded that 'the development of a richer and more flexible curriculum was a key factor in re-engaging young people in education, employment or training, and also in preventing 14–16 year olds from becoming disengaged'.

For some young people opportunities to engage in short, flexible programmes can support re-engagement with education, since short courses with clearly defined goals hold their interest and afford a sense of achievement (Ofsted, 2010a). The benefit of short courses leading to accreditation was a feature of some alternative provision in the schools involved in the School Exclusion Trial:

> The main thing we use AP [alternative provision] for is to engage them in mainstream ... We will do short courses where they achieve a qualification in a short period of time. They suddenly realise they can achieve something in six weeks and that has a huge knock-on effect in mainstream. In the food and nutrition course, we take them off timetable, we deliver the course in our Apple Mac room. The course is a mix of life skills plus and it's really effective. (Assistant head teacher)
>
> (IOE and NFER, 2014: 98)

In many educational institutions timetabling constraints, especially in relation to option choices at GCSE, can limit flexibility of provision. Lack of effective careers guidance can lead young people to taking inappropriate qualifications (see Chapter 8).

A contrasting approach to curriculum design is provided by The Pavilion School in Australia. The school offers an intensive literacy, numeracy and personal development programme for young people who have disengaged or have been excluded from mainstream education. Learning is framed within a student-centred approach and all young people follow an individually tailored education programme. Somewhat unusually, the school is structured so that students attend between six and ten hours of classes per week. Staff and students then work together to create a full timetable by organizing external services and educational programmes on an individual basis. For some students this could involve being linked to another accredited educational programme, while for others this might involve links to part-time work or to welfare and support agencies. In addition, electives are offered each week, rotating on a termly basis. These include art, personal training, boxing, music, drug and alcohol education, mental health awareness and anger management (Victoria Institute for Education, Diversity and Lifelong Learning, 2014).

As in the US and Australia, teachers and providers are increasingly looking towards different conceptions of the curriculum that will support the disengaged. One initiative is Big Picture Learning. Originating in the US in 1995, the mission is to educate one student at a time by personalizing each student's learning experience within a community of fellow learners. Underpinning the curriculum are three principles: (1) learning must be based on each student's interests and needs; (2) it must be relevant to the student and allow them to do real work in the real world; and (3) the student's growth and abilities must be measured by the quality of their work and how it changes them (Big Picture Learning, 2015). This unique learning programme is based around five competencies: empirical reasoning, quantitative reasoning, communication, social reasoning and personal qualities. Programmes based on the principles of Big Picture Learning also operate in Australia and the Netherlands (see Box 10.1).

BOX 10.1 BIG PICTURE LEARNING IN THE US

Students work in small groups of 15 to 18 students with a teacher, called an advisor, who guides the same group throughout their time in high school. Schools are small with only 140 students. Teachers work with students on an individual basis. Many young people are from disadvantaged backgrounds and are classified as at risk. Each student has a mentor outside the school who guides their internship. All students help create their own curriculum that expands and develops their interests. In addition young people attend an off-campus internship and have training in real-world work. Internships can take place anywhere, for instance, in a hospital, design studio, research lab or a bank. Students also engage in college courses. Big Picture Learning is based on problem-based learning whereby students solve day-to-day problems that relate to real-world situations.

Assessment differs to traditional approaches. Assessment criteria are individualized to the student and the real world standards of a project as evaluated by experts in the community. Assessments include public exhibitions, weekly check-in meetings with advisors, weekly journals, yearly presentation portfolios and transcripts.

(Big Picture Learning, 2015)

Informal learning

Informal learning opportunities, such as extra-curricular activities undertaken either outside the normal day in schools or colleges or within the community, offer the chance to engage with learning in non-academic contexts. Extra-curricular activities in schools and colleges include sports clubs, cheer leading, art and photography, drama, music, technology and volunteering. As well as such activities, community settings offer participation in church activities, youth clubs, scouts, guides, DJ-ing and radio production. While participation in extra-curricular activities can enhance the academic, social, physical and emotional growth of all students (Fredricks and Eccles, 2006), Davies *et al.* (2011) suggest that, for disengaged learners, it is just as important as formal learning. According to Everson and Millsap (2005), participation in extra-curricular activities is one of the few interventions that particularly benefit low-status, disadvantaged students who are less well served by traditional educational programmes. Voluntary participation is significant to engagement in extra-curricular activities.

Those involved in extra-curricular activities have been found to be more engaged in the classroom (Fredricks and Eccles, 2006). Extra-curricular activities provide the opportunity to develop positive support systems with peers and among staff, which in turn foster engagement in the classroom. Developing positive relationships with teachers is especially important for young people who are disengaged from education (see Chapter 11). Extra-curricular activities in the community offer a nurturing and family-like environment (Fredricks *et al.*, 2010). Disengaged young people express a need for extra-curricular activities such as boxing, martial arts, sport, cooking and wider life skills (Hartas, 2011).

Arts and sports

The role of the arts in education, particularly music, is well documented (see Hallam, 2015 for a review). Youth services and organizations use music and sound technology to good effect, often aimed at young people who may be disengaged from education, training or employment. The projects implemented range from those which provide space for young people to practise and perform, to those which enable them, through music, to explore themes such as identity or sub-cultures, or develop their technical skills of mixing, recording and producing (Hallam and Rogers, 2010). Among those regarded as NEET, music-making activities have been shown to increase motivation to engage in education, employment, or voluntary activity, promote a more positive attitude to learning and raise aspirations (Qa Research, 2012). In the studies reviewed, the young people developed a range of transferable skills such as team working, listening, reasoning and basic academic skills. There was also evidence of enhanced well-being and increased self-esteem and self-respect. Box 10.2 shows an example of how FE colleges can work with community organizations to offer arts-based education to engage young people.

> **Box 10.2 Collaboration between FE and the local community**
> Ofsted (2009) provides an example of collaboration between FE and the local community in which an 'Arts Depot' is incorporated within an FE college. This fully functioning community arts centre is equipped with two theatres, an exhibition gallery, rehearsal studios for music, dance and theatre and a disability arts and education forum. Ofsted describes this as a model of a shared-use arts space in which students behave and work to professional standards. According to Ofsted, this venue helps students develop realistic creative knowledge and skills more comprehensively than they would have had they studied solely in a college environment. Both the venue and the learning provision help to motivate young people, some of whom were previously disengaged.

Sport has the potential to reach large and diverse groups of young people and can play a valuable role in re-engaging those who are disengaged from education (France *et al.*, 2007). Research indicates that sports programmes facilitate an increased sense of belonging, respect for oneself and others, and a shared responsibility for learning (see Box 10.3).

> **BOX 10.3 GET STARTED PROGRAMME**
>
> Get Started is for UK residents aged 16–25 who are unemployed. Programmes last for five days and run throughout the country. Each course focuses on a theme such as sports, arts, music, science and technology. Football, cooking and fashion are among the most popular courses. At the end of each course there is an event to celebrate the achievements of the young people. All courses are run by qualified, professional experts. The aim of the programme is to enable young people to develop new skills, confidence and motivation. Get Started with Football in London and the South East, gives young people the opportunity to work with Reading Football Club and learn coaching skills from professionals. As a group participants work together to design and deliver a coaching session and the opportunity to achieve an FA Level 1 Award in Coaching Football. Get Started with Fashion, in partnership with Asos, provides young people with opportunities to improve their creative design skills and to complete and showcase their designs as part of a group challenge. Progression support is provided to all young people after the programme to help them find further employment and training opportunities. Costs for transport and lunch are covered.
>
> (Prince's Trust, 2015b)

Collaborative approaches to learning through outdoor activities

Students benefit from opportunities to work together. Where schools focus on learning collaboratively, they are more likely to have engaged students (Johnson, 2008). Students who have opportunities to interact and exchange ideas with each other during lessons are able to develop and refine their ideas, give and receive help, and in so doing evaluate other possibilities (Patrick *et al.*, 2007). Group work fosters relational learning where students learn from their peers as well as their teachers. Such approaches to learning promote the mastery of goals, academic efficacy and social efficacy with peers, and this in turn fosters the learning of self-regulatory strategies and achievement (Patrick *et al.*, 2007). Students working together collaboratively are more likely to focus on learning, more interested in the subject matter, and feel less anxious (Cushman and Rogers, 2008).

Outdoor and residential activities also promote collaborative learning. The SkillForce programme includes residential trips, sports, outdoor pursuits, community and environmental projects in addition to classroom work. Outdoor pursuits include camping, caving, rock climbing, orienteering and sailing. Community work includes making hedges, cutting down trees and tidying the landscape. Typically, the activities involve problem solving and all participants are required to keep records of the activities undertaken. They view the trips and activities positively, and so do the teaching staff in mainstream schools. The teamwork enhances their social skills and builds their confidence, seen to be important in re-engaging the young people.

> We do lots of fun activities. It makes everyone happy and they're really fun to do. We do bonding activities, partner stuff and loads of climbing and outdoor activities. The activities help to build up your confidence and help you to make new friends. They put you into groups with people that you don't really know and over time you get to know them. When we did high ropes that was fun. I felt quite nervous. There were people in front of me and behind me so I kept going. I was nervous because they were completely random people. I did know one person there. I didn't feel left out or anything. It felt good. (Year 9 student)
>
> (Hallam *et al.*, 2014a)

Outdoor activities give disengaged young people the chance to explore new activities in an environment that is totally different to the formality of the traditional classroom. They can be a soft-entry point for disengaged young people where they can build up confidence in the informal learning environment, which can lead to further education and training (see Box 10.4).

BOX 10.4 STRAMASH: OUTDOOR ACTIVITIES

Stramash is a social enterprise in Scotland to re-engage young people. The outdoor environment is used as an avenue for personal, social and economic development and provides disadvantaged young people and adults with the chance to experience the outdoors and learn new activities. A variety of day and residential courses are offered. Subsidized places are available to participants who cannot afford the fees. Since its onset Stramash has worked with over 5,000 people, averaging 35 users per week all year round.

(Scottish Government, 2010)

Embedding English and maths

Regardless of their educational context, disengaged young people often lack the literacy and numeracy skills they need to access and progress their education or employment opportunities. While there is wide variation in the characteristics of young people termed NEET and a lack of robust data in terms of literacy and numeracy levels, evidence suggests that many of them require support with basic skills (Hurry *et al.*, 2010; McNeil, 2008). The poor educational attainment of young people attending alternative educational provision also draws attention to the need to develop their maths and English (see Chapter 9). Concern over levels of literacy and numeracy among those who are disengaged from education is seen internationally. In Australia, the foundation skills courses offered to disengaged students by TAFE institutes have enabling students to acquire the literacy and numeracy skills required for further study or employment as a specific goal (Roberts and Wignall, 2010).

However, the difficulty is that the students who are disengaged from education often dislike maths and English, and are critical of the content of the lessons on the grounds that they do not enable them to make direct links with the requirements of real life (Hartas, 2011). Similarly, many young offenders have an unrealistic approach to functional skills. As one teacher put it: 'They want to become a plumber, but can't see the relevance of numeracy' (Hurry *et al.*, 2012: 26).

Too often the approaches to English and maths tend to focus on repetitive practice of low-level, rigidly sequenced skills in separate lessons that reflect a behavioural approach to learning and are characterized by surface learning. This approach seems neither challenging nor authentic, nor relevant to students' lives beyond the classroom. It seems hardly surprising that young people disengaged from education would not be motivated by this type of delivery.

An alternative approach is to embed the teaching of basic maths and English into vocational subjects so the students can develop these skills in a meaningful context. In the research undertaken in London prisons and YOIs (Hurry *et al.*, 2012) most staff agreed that literacy and numeracy were unpopular when taught quite separately from a vocational subject. Where functional skills were embedded, learning was more effective. The same was true of English for Speakers of Other Languages (ESOL). Where ESOL had been integrated into mainstream teaching, with specialist ESOL staff in support, ESOL learners were less isolated and made better progress. A more unusual but effective approach was to provide integrated pathways. In one YOI, integrated pathways included business, radio and music production and art, as well as the vocational areas of painting and decorating, DIY and brickwork, and these were supplemented with lessons in literacy and numeracy.

A further illustration is provided by Harper (2013) in her discussion of a lesson in bricklaying for boys aged 14 to 16 who were disengaged from education and were attending FE for three days a week. In common with many disengaged students, they all expressed a strong dislike for maths at school, since they did not see how it related to the world of work. The teacher drew on his strong vocational expertise to make the boys realize that they would not be able to lay bricks properly unless they could perform basic calculations. His explanations, related directly to the work context and were followed with lessons around tables in the workshop that concentrated on short, relevant calculations designed to improve students' numeracy skills. When they returned to the practical work, the teacher demanded high standards, regardless of the students' low prior attainment or their age, because he expected that all bricks had to be laid perfectly in accordance with industry standards.

While basic English and maths is often delivered in discrete settings, opportunities to integrate and embed maths and English into meaningful contexts may provide a way forward for disengaged students.

Technology

There is a growing evidence base that the effective use of technology in teaching and learning can engage disengaged students with education. Programmes that integrate technology into the delivery and teaching of the curriculum can promote student engagement (Walsh *et al.*, 2011). In a UK study by Ross (2009), 45 per cent of disengaged students reported liking Information and Communication Technology (ICT) a lot – this compared with just under 50 per cent of young people engaged with education. Among the NEET population, access to and the use of technology is high (Passey and Davies, 2010). From a pedagogic perspective, the use of technology enables students to apply their solutions to real-world problems with authentic audiences well beyond the boundaries of schools and colleges (Fullan and Longworthy, 2014). Used effectively, technology promotes a deep approach to learning in relation to the higher-order thinking skills that are involved and enables young people to work at their own pace in addition to collaborative working with others.

ICT evolves ever more quickly. Historically, perceptions of a digital divide raised concerns that the children of disadvantaged families were further disadvantaged by having no computers at home. The advent of Web 2.0 technologies and mobile devices has changed this. Even the highly disadvantaged young people own mobile phones (Walsh *et al.*, 2011). Mobiles offer a host of educational opportunities, for example electronic book readers, applications for composition, digital cameras and editing (Johnson *et al.*, 2011). They can assist with literacy by providing different forms of learning, such as auditory information and video modelling. There are indications that ICT can enable young people to overcome academic failure, since this is an area in which they may feel more competent and capable than in other academic subject domains.

The advent of new technologies requires that the positioning of ICT within education has to change; ICT is no longer just a subject choice or foundation skill. All young people expect technology to play a part in their daily lives and an integral role in their learning. Challenges arise when, as too often happens, teachers simply substitute technology for the usual tasks, such as reading about a topic on the internet and completing a worksheet in Word, instead of working from print and on to a printed worksheet. It could be no more than moving from copying from the board to copying from a website. Extensive copying of material is poor pedagogic practice for any learner. It fosters surface approaches to learning and the sense that facts are more important than understanding and that education is about transmission, with the power resting with the teacher. This reduces motivation and adds to feelings of boredom and the mismatch between their educational experience and their aspirations.

A further challenge relates to the affordances of Web 2.0 technologies and the use of social media and networking sites, for example MySpace, Facebook and YouTube. Schools often ban access to social networking sites and many Web 2.0 tools due to concerns about cyber bullying. Yet, as Rudd and Walker (2010) indicate, many young people use these tools outside school. This is yet another example of the mismatch of education and experience, as is the ambivalence around using gaming as an educational tool. Research has demonstrated, however, that video game classes could be important in keeping disengaged young people in education, in addition to helping plug a growing skills gap in the industry (Passey, 2012).

Despite these concerns, we see many positive illustrations of the use of technology to engage young people. In Victoria, Australia, the NETschool in Bendigo uses an online ICT offer to re-engage young people with education. Targeted at 15- to 19-year-olds who have left or are at risk of leaving education, it aims to reintegrate them into mainstream education, employment or training. Central to the approach is the recognition that each learner requires a new and different approach. Mentors and teachers work with them to develop individual learning plans centred on research-based learning. Research-based learning presents opportunities to develop the inquiry, research, higher-order thinking skills, and collaboration and communication skills they need to participate successfully in units of study or work placements. The learners work at home or in the online centre-based setting (see Box 10.5).

BOX 10.5 RESEARCH-BASED ONLINE LEARNING: NETSCHOOL, BENDIGO

Learners are placed in learning teams of ten. Each learner has their own workstation comprising a desk, ergonomic chair and desktop computer. Learners also have access to laptops, iPads and digital media equipment. Under the guidance of their mentor, each team identifies a need within their community and then researches the nature of the need. This includes identifying who is affected, what the impact is and the development of a plan to meet the need. At the end of each project the team deliver their ideas to the stakeholders. Each project provides young people with the opportunity to apply their skills to a topic of personal interest. As the project develops, mentors assist the learners to extend their skills and knowledge. New skills are taught according to individual need. Mentors evaluate each learner's growth in skills and knowledge and measure improvement against the Victorian Certificate of Applied Learning standards for Literacy and Numeracy, Work Related Skills and Personal Development Studies. In this way learners demonstrate competence against nationally recognized vocational standards.

(Bendigo Senior Secondary College, 2014)

An innovative use of technology in the UK is demonstrated by Notschool. net. Founded in 2005, Notschool.net is an online community of practice and differs from schools in terms of time, space, curriculum, ethos and location (Johnson *et al.*, 2013). Distinctive to this provision is that young people study a broad range of topics: the emphasis is on learning for life, not just for academic success. Eligibility for Notschool.net is restricted to long-term non-attenders, whether though illness, phobia, exclusion or disengagement. In contrast to much educational provision, some cultural groups such as

Travellers often fit the criteria because of their lifestyle. The learners study from home or a venue they feel comfortable in and at times that suit them. They choose their own curriculum and access learning through the online community, which makes extensive use of Web 2.0 tools.

Endnote

The curriculum offer and pedagogic approach to teaching and learning play a major part in preventing young people from disengaging from education and enabling others to return to education and training. Young people report wanting a more diverse, flexible curriculum that is relevant to their future lives and aspirations. Evidence of innovative practice is apparent in the imaginative use of digital technologies, the embedding of maths and English in authentic contexts, and in the students contributing to the decisions about their learning and the topics studied. Too often, though, young people at risk of disengagement or disengaged from education receive a routine, overly academic educational experience that is rooted in teacher-centred approaches. What work, however, are wider, enriched opportunities that are afforded by student-centred methods of teaching and learning that embrace constructivist approaches whereby the learner is the active maker of meaning.

Chapter summary

Young people benefit from engaging approaches to teaching and learning where the pedagogic practices build on their own experiences and aspirations.

Approaches to curricula and pedagogy that have proved successful include:

- use of collaborative group work
- active contributions from young people to establishing their own curriculum offer
- effective use of informal learning to re-engage students, held in community or outdoor settings
- interactive approaches to using technology that are rooted in the way young people use technology in their everyday lives
- authentic contexts for learning that relate to the world of work, particularly for the students who need support in developing maths and English.

Chapter 11

Teachers and teacher training

Arguably, one of the most important influences on young people's learning is the teacher. This chapter considers the importance of student–teacher relationships among those who are disengaged from education, their perceptions of teaching and learning and the importance of teachers holding high aspirations for all students. Consideration is given to teacher training, challenges to retention and how approaches to teacher training internationally are supporting a more diverse workforce that provides role models.

Context

The quality of teaching is the most crucial in-school factor in raising students' attainment and furthering educational progress (Sahlberg *et al.*, 2014). Put simply, 'the quality of an educational system cannot exceed the quality of its teachers' (Barber and Mourshed, 2007: 13). While the focus here is on the influence teachers have on the learning undertaken, it is important to acknowledge that other external factors are also influential. These include parents' educational attainment and engagement with their children's schooling, socio-economic disadvantage and health.

While not all those who are disengaged from education are from disadvantaged backgrounds, the effects of high-quality teaching are especially significant for this socio-economic group. Research indicates that over a single academic year, disengaged young people gain 1.5 years' worth of learning with very effective teachers, compared to 0.5 years with poorly performing teachers: this difference equates to a year of learning (Sutton Trust, 2011). It is of special concern that disadvantaged schools are not always staffed with the best teachers (OECD, 2012a) and that disadvantaged students, who mostly attend poorly resourced or isolated schools, are less likely to have access to highly qualified teachers (Gandara and Contreras, 2009).

Young people at risk of disengagement from education need a supportive and secure learning environment, where they feel valued, respected and safe and can experience positive relationships (Archer *et al.*, 2010; Ross, 2009). Where students work in an environment that is characterized by high expectations, readiness to invest effort and good student–teacher relationships, they tend to achieve more highly. Disengaged students learn more and have fewer disciplinary problems when they feel that their teachers are dedicated to their success (OECD, 2012a).

Teaching: International perspectives

Attainment

Governmental recognition of global economic competitiveness and the shift from industrial to knowledge economies draw attention to the role of education in developing economic competitiveness (Sahlberg and Boce, 2010). On the basis of the results achieved in international educational comparative studies, the role and responsibilities of schools and teachers in preserving or improving positions is considered – a situation common to many countries (Power, 2007). This is accompanied by measures used to gauge the effectiveness and thus the accountability of teachers (Gray and Colucci-Gray, 2010).

The emphasis on performativity, as illustrated by the use of ability grouping, tracking and setting, impacts on all pupils. Teachers adopt different teaching styles according to the ability level of the group they are teaching so that lower ability groups experience a restricted range of activities, more structured work and more rehearsal and repetition. For young people disengaged from education, the differential expectations their teachers hold may compound their disengagement. They themselves report that too much copying off the board or from a text book contributes to their disengagement (Duffy and Elwood, 2013; Lloyd-Jones *et al.*, 2010).

While the policy focus on achieving qualifications is understandable, it ignores a holistic approach to education in which there may be other significant outcomes such as personal growth and well-being (Hodkinson *et al.*, 2007). Students who are at risk of disengagement or who have disengaged from education are particularly in need of opportunities to develop self-esteem and their confidence in learning (see Chapters 5, 6, 7 and 9).

Retention

In many countries, teacher turnover is high. In the UK, it is problematic in inner city schools, where the turnover of staff is higher than elsewhere. Teacher attrition is particularly significant in areas of disadvantage, as it may be a factor in reproducing disadvantage (Mills and Gale, 2009). In the US, about a third of all teachers leave the profession, half of them within five years. Hard-to-staff schools such as high-poverty urban schools lose 22 per cent of their teachers every year. Low-poverty schools experience a turnover rate of almost 13 per cent (AFT, 2007).

Head teachers in disadvantaged schools report that, although they have lower student–teacher ratios, they have less experienced and qualified teachers (OECD, 2012a). Teachers are less likely to favour schools in rural and remote settings, along with schools with higher proportions of disadvantaged children and children from minority ethnic and language backgrounds (OECD, 2005).

The range of experience and skills required of teachers working with disengaged students may act as a disincentive for them to continue working with disengaged students and deter potential new teachers (KPMG, 2009), but this is not always the case. Educators working in YOIs, for example show positive motivations to work with disengaged students and have altruistic reasons for taking up this work (Rogers *et al.*, 2014).

Teaching disengaged students

Teaching is a challenging occupation. Classrooms are demanding, busy places in which to work. They are multifaceted, as the children have different goals, interests, purposes and experiences, all operating simultaneously. Teaching is a complex undertaking, involving classroom management, lesson preparation and organization of teaching and learning activities, creating and maintaining a certain ethos and evaluating and giving feedback (Hendriks *et al.*, 2010). However one views the role of the teacher, two points are worth making. First, teachers cannot learn for their students. Second, teachers can support student learning in many ways. Effective teachers make a significant difference to student learning, motivation and achievement.

Disengaged students may behave in challenging ways in the classroom. In England, disaffected students were defined as those who displayed one or more of the following characteristics:

- regularly non-compliant, but not aggressive or threatening
- causing repeated low-level disruptions;
- regularly disruptive, challenging or both;
- subject to recurring fixed-term exclusions;
- absent for 20 per cent or more of the available school sessions in the year;
- were quiet and withdrawn and uninterested in most lessons.

(Ofsted, 2008: 4)

In addition, many of those disengaged from education arrive in secondary school without basic skills in literacy and numeracy. All teachers need to take this diversity into account in the design and delivery of their teaching (OECD, 2012a).

Disengaged students, particularly those who drop out of education, do less homework, put less effort into school, participate less in school activities and have more discipline problems. Generally, the more successful and enjoyable young people find learning, the more likely they are to continue engaging with it and the more likely they are to persist when they face difficulties (Hallam, 2005). Successful engagement in learning is crucial for students to achieve qualifications and pathways into further study and work (see Chapter 10).

Teachers influence student motivation and achievement (Montalvo *et al.*, 2007). They have the major responsibility for engaging students through their choice of teaching strategies, the techniques they employ to motivate students and the pedagogical relationships they establish (Leach *et al.*, 2014). Their work entails enabling students to have some control over their learning and choice of activities, setting work at an appropriate level, giving praise as appropriate, acknowledging the role that emotions play in learning, recognizing and rewarding different levels of prior knowledge and establishing a focus on mastery rather than performance goals (Hallam, 2005).

Disengaged students perspectives on teaching

Internationally, research indicates that over time students become less engaged with aspects of learning in school. While many concerns arise from the lack of relevance of the curriculum offer (see Chapter 10), other issues relate directly to the experience of teaching. In New Zealand, for example, students became more critical of teaching as they progressed through secondary school. They noted work set at an inappropriate level of difficulty, perceived learning to be dry and boring and found the school's environment not conducive to learning (Ministry of Education, 2008).

Young people who are absent from school for whatever reason face difficulties due to the accumulation of work that is missed. The students report that the further behind they fall, the less likely they are to feel able to succeed in class, and this in turn makes them more likely to create trouble and be sent out, so miss even more (Lloyd-Jones *et al.*, 2010). Students who miss lessons need opportunities to catch up on missed work.

The students themselves have clear views about which aspects of teaching and learning they find engaging. They value opportunities to relate to and have positive relationships with teachers, more hands-on and practical work, active participation in the classroom, varied lessons and teachers who don't appear stressed, are more flexible and do not dominate the learning with too much teacher input (Baird *et al.*, 2011). Young people also express the wish for positive and consistent recognition, particularly for good behaviour (Nuttall and Woods, 2013). The most frequently cited factor contributing to their disengagement is poor relationships with teachers.

Although the use of the term disengagement from education implies that young people are not interested in learning, research indicates the contrary. Many young people believe it important to gain qualifications to help them achieve their aspirations (Lloyd-Jones *et al.*, 2010; Duffy and Elwood, 2013). Even when they are not on track to gain any GCSEs or equivalent, they aspire to gain employment that requires qualifications. Thus there is often a mismatch between the students' aspirations and the ways they appear in the classroom. Young people in alternative educational provision or in YOIs also wish to learn and gain qualifications.

Relationships with teachers

The relationships young people build and develop with their teachers are an important contributor to the school climate (Thapa *et al.*, 2013). Positive relationships with teachers enable the building of rapport, thus facilitating interaction and communication and nurturing students' well-being. These in turn lead to positive behaviour and higher standards. Through positive relationships students learn about their beliefs, their views of learning and the values they need to operate well in an academic environment. Effective student–teacher relationships offer help and emotional support with learning. These findings hold for all young people.

For those who are disengaged from education, supportive, trusting relationships with teachers are especially important. Positive relationships where students feel fairly treated and are given appropriate praise, where they feel safe, respected and understood can contribute to their engagement (Ross, 2009). When students learn to trust their teacher, they may begin to take chances and invest effort in a task (Strahan, 2008). A positive relationship with even one teacher or support worker makes a difference to how disengaged young people feel about school (Lyche, 2010; Archer *et al.*, 2010).

The impact on the student–teacher relationship can be positive or negative. Positive student–teacher relationships foster engagement, but a breakdown in relationships can be part of a downward spiral of disengagement

(Callanan *et al.*, 2009). Students perceive negative relationships with teachers as a contributing factor to their disengagement (Lumby, 2011; Lloyd-Jones *et al.*, 2010). Many of the disengaged rate their ability to engage and learn in a subject on the nature of their relationship with their teacher, and those who do not have a positive relationship with their teacher are more likely to disengage from the subject she teaches (KPMG, 2009).

Pivotal to the quality of the student–teacher relationship is the matter of respect. Those who disengage from education frequently perceive their teacher to have little respect for them. Students talk, for instance, about their sense that teachers look down on them. Another oft-cited concern is feeling as if they are being treated like kids or babies, particularly because of the way their teachers speak to them (Lloyd-Jones *et al.*, 2010, Duffy and Elwood, 2013).

The students who feel ignored by or unimportant to teachers are the ones who report higher levels of boredom, disengagement and unhappiness. Researchers have suggested that the responses from young people labelled as disengaged may actually relate to their frustration about the dynamics within the classroom, which seem impossible to change or challenge, rather than disengagement *per se* (Hartas, 2011).

When young people are disengaged from education, teachers need to take time to listen to them, be patient and consistent in their support (te Riele, 2014). This was exemplified in the approach taken by SkillForce in developing their relationships with the students on an alternative educational programme (Hallam *et al.*, 2003). The young people felt they were treated with respect and like adults: 'SkillForce staff and teachers are nothing like each other. If you treat the SkillForce staff with respect then they treat you like adults with respect. Teachers aren't like that'. These young people then applied the knowledge and skills they acquired in SkillForce to their relationships with other teachers: 'Like if you respect them they respect you back. So you try and do it with other teachers and see if they respect you back. Sometimes they do and sometimes they don't' (Student) (Hallam *et al.*, 2003: 47). They found it important that instructors took time to explain things to the young people and to offer support:

> Say you didn't understand it, then they'd help you and they'd explain it again, whereas if you're in school and you don't understand it some teachers can actually turn around and say 'I've already said it once, work it out for yourselves'. So really it ain't learning you. (Student)
>
> (Hallam *et al.*, 2003: 48)

High aspirations, attainment and behaviour

While students who are disengaged from education benefit from positive relationships with teachers, this is not to say that they should not be presented with challenges in relation to either their learning or their poor behaviour. Regarding attainment, it is important that teachers establish an environment where students are not afraid to fail (Lloyd-Jones *et al.*, 2010). This is especially important for those who have had few experiences of success in education. In order to help motivate and re-engage young people with education, teachers need to provide young people with opportunities for success.

All those attending SkillForce were provided with occasions for success. This was the first time that some of the participants had ever received a certificate. The programmes were based around work-related learning, with everyone working towards an array of certificates and awards. In one pilot programme, the students worked towards Wider Key Skills, Certificate in Personal Effectiveness (COPE) Level 2, the BTEC Public Services Extended Certificate and GCSE Maths. In another programme, the participants worked towards GCSE Maths, the Level 1 Uniformed Services Diploma, the Level 1 Sports Leaders Award, as well as following drugs awareness and first aid courses. Their parents commented on the qualifications their children had acquired:

> He's got first aid and he's got a certificate for misuse of substance – which those two alone will be brilliant for him for the job that he is going on ... like he has got to do health and safety, first aid ... all those sort of things. They use a lot of chemicals on site, so that misuse of substance is a good thing for him to have. So really, this has just given him a little step up the ladder with his job really, which he wouldn't really get until he was actually working. So it's been good. (Parent)
>
> (Hallam *et al.*, 2012: 28)

It is relevant that even where ability grouping is not adopted, there are concerns that teachers, albeit with good intentions, adjust their educational expectations of those who are disengaged from education, because they rate well-being as more important than learning (te Riele, 2014). But this has the potential to disadvantage the students, especially if they are not offered challenging tasks or opportunities. Low expectations influence the nature of the curriculum offer, the quality of instruction the teachers provide and the provision of resources. In turn, this can have a negative impact on the self-esteem of the students, their aspirations and their future motivation to learn.

Students appreciate clear boundaries regarding behaviour (Lloyd-Jones *et al.*, 2010) and knowing the consequences for poor behaviour. Drawing on their research in Australia, Mills and McGregor (2010) commented that the issue for young people was not the rules, but how they were enforced. In contrast to their experiences of school, the alternative provision rules were applied in the context of dialogue with the students. In successive evaluations of SkillForce, improvements in behaviour were found to be due to the consistency and stability of the teaching environment. SkillForce programmes had a clear set of boundaries and rules that had to be followed. The rules were enforced – not by shouting at students, but by speaking to them calmly:

> Students do not get away with things but they are spoken to at an appropriate time, i.e. not at the moment when they might be kicking off but when they are calmer. There are some schools where if a pupil swears under their breath they will be chased through the school corridors by a member of staff to catch them. They will then be excluded. SkillForce is really clear about appropriate consequences of actions. They do not shout at pupils. (Instructor)
>
> (Hallam *et al.*, 2013)

As Mills and McGregor (2010) suggest, the approach taken to managing behaviour in alternative education could be useful for mainstream schools, too. The mutual respect between staff and students influenced the approach taken to dealing with poor behaviour and enabled the students to maintain their dignity.

Teachers as role models

The way the teacher is perceived is extremely important. Young learners need to be able to identify with their teachers as role models. Positive relationships with teachers and other adult role models are crucial in preventing disengagement from school (Nelson and O'Donnell, 2012) and can help pupils stay on track with their learning (Bielby *et al.*, 2012). Research into provision within YOIs draws attention to the point that the disengaged youngsters often lack appropriate role models. As one education manager stated: '[Young offenders] don't want to be taught by their aunts or well-meaning older adults. They want to be able to relate to young men, and preferably to young black men with whom they share an understanding of a culture' (Hurry *et al.*, 2012: 27). To put this in context, just under 26 per cent of the prison population in June 2014, or 21,937 prisoners, were from a minority ethnic group (Prison Reform Trust, 2014), although this group forms only 10 per cent of the general population. Ten per cent of the British national prison population are black, which is significantly higher than the 2.8 per cent of black Britons in the general population. This suggests that black teaching staff should be more highly represented in prisons if young offenders are to be given more positive role models.

SkillForce instructors are mainly ex-services personnel with diverse life experiences, and they provide positive role models for the disengaged young participants in their programmes. They were respected because their credentials related to the real world (Hallam *et al.*, 2014b). School staff referred to the importance of having male role models and commented on the way SkillForce staff developed positive relationships with young people who were sometimes difficult to reach:

> I think the SkillForce team are particularly good at developing relationships with young people that are positive and role-modelling positive relationships and role-modelling that resilience and that independent thinking, listening to each other and respecting each other.
>
> (Hallam *et al.*, 2014b)

Teacher training

Initial Teacher Education (ITE) is the first phase of the professional cycle of a teacher, part of the professional continuum of learning and expertise. Teachers develop their skills and competencies with their experience in the classroom and through engaging with continuing professional development. There is concern about the number of unqualified teachers in academies and free schools in England following the coalition government's decision in 2012 to permit these institutions to recruit teaching staff who have not taught in state schools before and do not have qualified teacher status (QTS). Between 2012 and 2013 the number of teachers without QTS rose from 14,800 full-time equivalent to 17,100 (DfE, 2014e).

The development of inclusive thinking and practice

Most countries set out common expectations about the knowledge, understanding and skills that new teachers should have. In relation to pupils who are disengaged from education, expectations are often couched in terms of teachers responding to the needs and strengths of all pupils and adopting teaching and learning approaches that enable all pupils to be taught effectively (see Box 11.1 for an example). There is, however, variability in the provision of ITE. In Germany, teachers are ill-equipped to deal with students from an immigrant background (OECD, 2011). In England, the Carter Review (2015) identified the following gaps in ITE courses: subject knowledge, subject-specific pedagogy, behaviour management, assessment, and SEN and disabilities.

BOX 11.1: ENGLAND ITE STANDARD 5
Adapt teaching to respond to the strengths and needs of all pupils:

- Know when and how to differentiate appropriately, using approaches which enable pupils to be taught effectively
- Have a secure understanding of how a range of factors can inhibit pupils' ability to learn, and how best to overcome these
- Demonstrate an awareness of the physical, social and intellectual development of children, and know how to adapt teaching to support pupils' education at different stages of development
- Have a clear understanding of the needs of all pupils including those with special educational needs; those of high ability; those with English as an additional language; those with disabilities; and be able to use and evaluate distinctive teaching approaches to engage and support them.

(DfE, 2012b: 8)

By contrast, in Finland all teachers are trained in diagnosing students with learning difficulties and in adapting their teaching to the various learning needs of their students (OECD, 2011). Similarly, all teachers in Sweden receive specific preparation to teach students from diverse backgrounds (OECD, 2012a).

Role models: A more diverse workforce

Young people who are disengaged from education need to be given opportunities to be taught or supported by adults who provide effective role models. The populations under-represented in ITE and the teaching workforce in many countries are often the groups most underserved by the education system (Villegas and Davis, 2007). Some progress has been made in the UK recruiting ethnic minority trainees, up from 7 per cent in secondary schools in 1998 to 14 per cent in 2011 (MacBeath, 2011). More could still be done about recruitment, and about recruiting teachers who have disabilities. One such initiative is the Teacher Pathways Program run by Portland State University in the US, which seeks to increase diversity within the workforce (see Box 11.2).

Box 11.2 US: Teacher Pathways Program

The Teacher Pathways Program at Portland State University (PSU) is a student support program for diverse undergraduate students and career-changers interested in becoming a teacher. It provides teaching career pathways and support for culturally diverse students interested in becoming a teacher and recruits diverse PSU undergraduates, community college students, instructional assistants and other career-changers. A specific programme objective is to increase and support the pipeline of culturally and linguistically diverse students interested in teaching careers.

(Portland State University, 2015)

Within the context of VET it is also important that teachers, as role models, are experts in their vocational field. Teach Too, a recent initiative in FE in England, aims to encourage occupational experts from industry to spend time teaching their occupational expertise to others and to contribute to curriculum development, while continuing to work. In essence this relates to the practice of teachers and trainers of drawing on up-to-date industry experience to provide excellent education and training.

The recruitment of high-quality teachers into disadvantaged schools

Despite the large influence of teachers on student performance, disadvantaged schools are not always staffed with the best teachers. I do not suggest that disadvantaged schools only cater for disengaged students or that such students only attain poor qualifications. However, policies must raise teacher quality for disadvantaged schools and students by taking the following steps: delivering targeted teacher education to ensure that teachers acquire the skills and knowledge they need for working in schools with disadvantaged students, providing mentoring programmes for beginner teachers, developing working conditions to improve teacher effectiveness and increase teacher retention, and developing financial and career incentives to attract and retain good teachers in disadvantaged schools (OECD, 2012a).

The Career Change Program in Australia, which ran until 2012, sought to recruit qualified professionals such as engineers, scientists, mathematicians, trades people and IT experts to become trainee teachers. Participants attended a preparatory summer school before entering the classroom the following school year. They underwent a school-based induction programme and received ongoing support from mentor teachers (Gopinathan *et al.*, 2008).

Teach First, founded in 2002, is an English version of the US programme Teach for America. It is an employment-based route with the distinctive objective of placing highly qualified graduates in challenging schools. A key aspect is their work with schools to improve students' aspirations, experiences and achievements. Teach First has a specific remit to address educational disadvantage by working in challenging and complex urban schools (see Box 11.3).

Box 11.3 Teach First

Teach First employs a rigorous approach to selection, involving two stages, including a day-long assessment centre. Applicants are assessed against eight areas of competency, including: humility, respect and empathy, subject knowledge, leadership, problem solving and resilience. School staff are used in making assessments and a range of assessors observe and evaluate each candidate. Teach First works in collaboration with a number of universities. In 2015 Teach First aims to recruit over 2,000 teachers to work in schools serving low-income communities in England and Wales.

Fundamental to the success of Teach First is the recruitment of a substantial number of graduates who would not otherwise have become teachers, and who have good degrees from elite universities and outstanding personal qualities; and the short- and long-term contribution to the staffing of challenging schools in disadvantaged areas.

(Hutchings *et al.*, 2006)

Endnote

Teachers play a pivotal role in motivating students to engage with education. For those at risk of disengagement or disengaged from education, this is even more important since the student–teacher relationship can impact in positive or negative ways. It is of fundamental importance that young people disengaged from education are treated with respect and that teachers hold high aspirations for their achievement. Sadly, many young people who are disengaged from education report being shouted at and undervalued in the classroom. In addition, they often have the least experienced or less competent teachers. Governments internationally need to ensure that good teachers are attracted to working with disengaged and disadvantaged young people and that strategies are in place to engage a more diverse workforce in the profession.

Chapter summary

Positive relationships with disengaged students and their teachers indicate that this occurs when teachers:

- listen to young people and involve them in decisions about their learning
- interact in a responsive and respectful manner
- hold high expectations of their students
- take time to get to know their students, their backgrounds and interests, emotional strengths and academic level
- rarely show irritability towards their students and deal with behaviour in an appropriate manner.

For positive relationships to be fostered with young people disengaged from education, it is important that teachers act as role models, that the teaching workforce is representative of the diversity of the student population, and that the best teachers work with young people disengaged from education.

Governments worldwide need to ensure that ITE is of the highest quality to support trainee teachers to work with diverse groups of students. Particular attention needs to be paid to increasing the diversity of the teaching profession.

Part Four

Overview

Chapter 12

Overview

This chapter considers how all those involved with the education and training of 11- to 19-year-olds in the developed world can best challenge disengagement from education and help break cycles of intergenerational disadvantage. The chapter sets out the accountability and responsibility of government, policymakers, employers, educators, teachers and lecturers in preventing young people from disengaging from education, and identifies approaches to re-engage young people who have dropped out of education.

Introduction

Education is fundamental in promoting economic development and the social and personal welfare of individuals. The future opportunities for individuals and their children are significantly influenced by participation and engagement in education and training. The educational attainment of young people, especially at upper secondary level, strongly affects their adult earnings, their likelihood of employment, and whether their own children will be in poverty in the future (HM Government, 2014). Young people moving into adulthood without adequate skills and qualifications face increasing marginalization. Particularly vulnerable are those who, for various reasons disengage from education or drop out of it altogether. Young offenders, who are educated within the secure estate, face additional challenges in their reintegration into the community.

Many studies in the developed world, including those of a longitudinal nature, illustrate how advantage and disadvantage are transmitted down the generations. Research explores the relationships between childhood factors, for instance the parents' education level and employment status and their educational attainment, as well as the extent to which these factors predict poverty in later life.

Education is a major contributor to the intergenerational transmission of disadvantage and is regularly identified as the key mechanism explaining intergenerational income mobility (Serafino and Tonkin, 2014). Most childhood factors associated with the intergenerational transmission of poverty operate by impacting on the child's educational outcomes (D'Addio,

2007; HM Government, 2014). Poor educational attainment is associated with a higher risk of dropping out of education (Lyche, 2010). Adults in the EU who have poor qualifications are more likely to be in poverty than the more educated (Grundiza and Lopez Vilaplana, 2013).

Intergenerational persistence

The transmission of disadvantage in relation to income, occupations and education shows little mobility across generations. This, however, masks differences across countries as in some the extent of association between parents and their children is less marked.

Educational outcomes persist across generations for a range of reasons (D'Addio 2007; Guerin, 2014; Serafino and Tonkin, 2014). What most heightens the risk of a poor child growing up to be a poor adult, is a child's educational attainment (HM Government 2014; Serafino and Tonkin, 2014). Other factors such as low parental qualifications, parental ill health, child ill health, the home environment, children's non-cognitive skills, and childhood poverty also influence educational attainment (HM Government, 2014). In the UK, young people with a low level of educational attainment are almost five times as likely as the well-educated to be in poverty now and 11 times as likely to be severely materially deprived (Serafino and Tonkin, 2014). Worklessness also contributes to intergenerational disadvantage. Fourteen-year-olds who grow up in a workless household are approximately 1.5 times as likely to be in poverty compared with those where one adult is working (Serafino and Tonkin, 2014).

The persistence of attainment levels across generations also varies according to the level of the parents' education. A recent study asked adults aged 25 to 59 across Europe about their level of education and that of their parents, and compared the two (Grundiza and Lopez Vilaplana, 2013). Of those respondents whose parents had a low level of education, defined as at most lower secondary education, 34 per cent also had a low level of education. Forty-eight per cent had a medium level of education (upper secondary) and 18 per cent a high level (tertiary). Eight per cent of respondents whose parents had a medium level of education, had a low level of education, 59 per cent medium, and 33 per cent high. Among respondents where parents had a high level of education, 3 per cent had a low level of education, 33 per cent medium and 63 per cent high (Grundiza and Lopez Vilaplana, 2013). How the level of educational attainment persists from generation to generation is very evident.

Differences can be seen, however, in the transmission of intergenerational disadvantage across countries (D'Addio, 2007; Serafino and Tonkin, 2014; HM Government, 2014). In some countries, such as the Czech Republic, Slovakia and Poland, 75 per cent or over of adults whose parents had low levels of education moved to a medium level of education (Grundiza and Lopez Vilaplana, 2013). However, persistence of a low level of education was apparent among half or more of the respondents in Malta, Portugal, Luxembourg, Spain and Italy.

Intergenerational earnings mobility, the extent to which the economic status of children differs from that of their parents, also varies from country to country. Some countries have much higher levels of intergenerational mobility than others. For instance, according to D'Addio (2007), less than 20 per cent of the difference in parental incomes was passed on to children in Australia, Canada and some Nordic countries. By contrast, between 40 and 50 per cent of income status was passed on in Italy, the UK and the US.

Two conclusions are worth drawing from these data. First, mobility in relation to earnings and levels of educational attainment is lower at the bottom of the distribution, thus strengthening the transmission of poverty across generations. Second, the differences seen in levels of intergenerational mobility across countries indicate that it is possible to develop systems that support individuals in raising their aspirations and increasing mobility.

Government

One of the main objectives of social policy is to break the cycle of disadvantage across generations. Greater equality of opportunity affords the chance to reduce the need for welfare support, encourage greater social cohesion, and make use of the potential of all individuals, thus increasing economic efficiency (D'Addio, 2007). Launched in 2010, the European 2020 Strategy, for instance, aims to 'turn the EU into a smart, sustainable and inclusive economy delivering high levels of employment, productivity and social cohesion' (European Commission, 2010c: 3). Two of the five flagship targets are pertinent here: the first, which is to reduce the number of early school leavers to below 10 per cent, and the second, which is to lift at least 20 million people out of the risk of poverty or social exclusion. In 2012, the percentage of early school leavers was 12.7 and it is doubtful whether the EU will reach the 10 per cent target by 2020 (European Commission, 2014). The target on poverty reduction is out of reach, due partly to the economic crisis. The number of people at risk of poverty or social exclusion in the EU has increased to over 118 million in 2010, over 121 million in 2011, and over 124 million in 2012 (European Commission, 2014). There is much that needs to be done.

International comparisons of education systems show that it is possible to combine quality with equity so that most young people, regardless of their personal or socio-economic circumstances, are afforded the opportunity to attain high level skills (OECD, 2012a). While almost all countries view the reduction of school failure as evidenced by dropout as a high priority, educational systems and practices differ, and not all support young people who are disengaged from education, as can be seen by practices of grade repetition, rigid institutional selection, early streaming and ability grouping.

High-quality teaching is the key to breaking the cycle of disadvantage, and yet all too often disadvantaged schools are not staffed with the most skilled teachers. Critical also is the relevance of the curricula to the world of work and the need to make academic and vocational pathways equivalent. If we are to engage young people at risk of dropping out of education, it is important that they are given choices about their educational pathways and that all pathways afford clear opportunities for progression. In too many countries, including the UK and Canada, the dominance of the academic curriculum over vocational pathways needs to be addressed. While this might necessitate a revision of vocational provision, evidence suggests that successful vocational qualifications utilize robust assessment procedures that adopt an outcomes-based design that focuses on competency-based completion rather than time-based completion. Successful provision also needs to include basic skills training that integrates literacy and numeracy into the vocational and work-based training. Such provision allows better articulation between higher level vocational awards and higher education systems (OECD, 2014c; 2014d).

In relation to education and training, governments can ensure that:

- the status of teaching as a profession is valued, the churn of teachers in challenging educational environments is minimized and good teachers are employed in disadvantaged educational institutions
- recruitment into the teaching profession attracts high-quality trainee teachers and a diverse workforce that is representative of the population of young people
- good education is available for all young people wherever they live and regardless of their level of need and the context in which their education takes place
- high-quality education is placed higher on the agenda for those within the secure estate and attention is paid to the continuation of education when the young offenders return to the community

- the over-emphasis on attainment as manifest by international league tables does not detract from an emphasis on the personalization of learning
- the curriculum provided is relevant, offers flexibility of approach and is matched to the needs and aspirations of the learners
- the infrastructure is in place for ensuring that young people have access to ongoing developments in digital technologies
- national assessment procedures are motivating and emphasize mastery rather than performance goals
- educational institutions offer an environment that is safe, supportive and conducive to learning
- appropriate support is available for young people at risk of disengaging from education and for those who have already disengaged from education
- meaningful second-chance opportunities are provided to all those who are disengaged from education with clear progression pathways
- educational institutions that are in difficulties are offered sufficient support to bring about change.

Employer engagement

Employer engagement is central to the positioning of an appropriate vocational offer for young people, particularly those disengaged from education. This obviously includes vocational qualifications, traineeships and apprenticeships, but it goes beyond this to include giving young people opportunities to gain work experience, to seek careers guidance, and to engage in entrepreneurship and enterprise activities.

Much could be done to extend the provision of apprenticeships or pre-apprenticeships by integrating the apprenticeship system within formal schooling, as is the case in Australia, France and Germany. The number of apprenticeships in the UK offered at Level 3 rather than Level 2 should be increased so that qualifications have higher credibility and link directly to employment opportunities and progression.

Dropout rates remain quite high in apprenticeship and pre-apprenticeship programmes. Schools, colleges and employers need to work in partnership to address this.

Employers also have a key role to play in fostering vocational skill among lecturers, practitioners and teachers who deliver vocational training so that all those engaged in teaching remain up to date with industry standards and the use of technology.

Educational institutions

All those working in schools, colleges, alternative educational provision and the criminal justice system can make a difference to the lives of young people who are at risk of disengaging with education or who have already disengaged. Creating a positive educational environment in which all young people receive equity of opportunity and treatment is essential.

Those with leadership and management responsibilities hold a pivotal role. Strong and positive leadership is crucial in all educational settings, as is the fostering of a collaborative ethos where staff, students and families feel valued and listened to. It is the responsibility of management to ensure that all staff have the opportunity to continue their professional development, that new teaching staff are supported in the development of their practice, and that staff with mentoring responsibilities for new teachers are given remission for this work.

Responses to young people who are at risk of disengaging have to be proactive rather than reactive. Clear policies and guidance for staff working with young people who are disengaged from education need to be developed through consultation, systematically implemented, monitored for effectiveness, and reviewed and changed where necessary.

The ethos of the institution should support students to develop their learning by giving them opportunities to succeed, and by being consistent in its approach to poor behaviour. Staff should have the freedom to develop imaginative approaches to teaching and learning. Taking risks is an important part of learning for both the students and their teachers. Having the confidence to take risks is key to engaging with learning.

It is essential that the educational ethos is inclusive. Too often the students disengaged from education are stereotyped as having little ability and potential because their teachers and lecturers hold low expectations of them. A positive ethos, conveying to all students that they are valued and respected and that they can achieve, is fundamentally important.

Teaching staff

Teachers play a pivotal role in motivating students to engage with education, training and learning. Their choice of teaching strategies, the organization of activities, the feedback that they give, and the relationships they establish with young people strongly influence student engagement. For young people disengaged with education, the quality of the student–teacher relationship is especially important. Too often they have negative relationships with their teachers that are frequently characterized by a lack of respect. To foster positive relationships, teachers need to treat all young people with respect, provide opportunities for success whereby learning is scaffolded appropriately, hold high aspirations for all their students, engage students in decisions about their learning, take time to get to know them, and act as role models. Young people who are making educational decisions about their future need to be given high-quality, impartial careers advice and guidance.

Curricula issues

Evident throughout this book is the young people's perception that the irrelevance of the curriculum on offer contributes to disengagement. While many governments do determine the overall curriculum content and assessment regime, teachers can be more proactive in tailoring the curriculum to meet the needs of their students by understanding the requirements of those who have become disengaged. Wider curricula are needed, plus better vocational provision. But teachers also need to provide authentic contexts for learning so that their students can make connections between classroom activities and their application in the real world. This seems especially the case for the young people who struggle with literacy and numeracy.

Greater use could be made of informal learning opportunities and extra-curricular activities in school, the community, and through links with industry. These sources of learning can have a greater impact on the disengaged young person's aspirations and beliefs than the more formal academic learning presented in the classroom. Informal learning opportunities can provide soft entry points back into education and training whereby young people can develop their confidence as a learner.

Pedagogy

Many young people disengaged from education report teacher-centred approaches to teaching and learning that emphasize performance goals and create a competitive approach to attainment, and that they have little choice in how and what they learn. Frequent testing and the practice of grade repetition also contribute to disengagement. Greater attention needs to be paid to student-centred approaches to teaching and learning that involve the disengaged students in the construction of their learning. Students need to be offered a more personalized approach to learning and afforded opportunities for applied or hands-on learning. Imaginative pedagogic practice in the use of digital technologies to re-engage young people with education seems under-developed and this reveals a missed opportunity to bridge the divide between the way young people use technology and how this translates within the traditional classroom.

Support for the individual

Disengagement from education falls along a continuum. Young people disengage from education and training for many different reasons. Those who have dropped out will require varied levels of support to enable them to re-engage with education or to return to training. For some young people disengagement will be transitory, and short-term interventions and strategies for coping may be sufficient. Others might be better suited to an alternative educational environment where class sizes are usually smaller and the students have opportunities to address the barriers to engagement they face and gradually return to mainstream education. Young people serving custodial sentences have much to contend with. In common with many of those who are disengaged with education, they often have poor literacy and numeracy skills and need support in developing them. A minority of young people will become NEET and may need intensive support to re-engage with education.

Many of those who are disengaged from education do in fact hold positive aspirations and ambitions for their future. Interventions to support them should build on their hopes and interests rather than perpetuating deficit notions of ability and disadvantage.

Teacher training

Given the critical role teachers have in motivating and engaging young people with education, the importance of selecting and training new teachers cannot be overstated. Countries vary in how much prominence teacher education programmes place on preparing trainee teachers to teach students from diverse backgrounds and how much time is devoted to understanding and working with students who have learning difficulties or SEN and to developing inclusive thinking and practice. Inequalities exist in the recruitment of trainee teachers from under-represented groups, resulting in a lack of diversity in the workforce. This applies particularly to those who are disengaged from education and who would benefit from adult role models to whom they can relate.

For disengaged students to have real opportunities to succeed in education and training, greater attention needs to be paid to inclusive approaches to education within teacher training programmes. Those responsible for selecting trainee teachers need to revisit selection procedures to ensure that the workforce is more representative of the diversity of the student population.

Families

Many young people who are disengaged from education will need the support of adults, including their families, to succeed in education. Families play a fundamental role in their children's education. Their aspirations, their beliefs about education, their ability to provide resources to support education, the discussions they have about educational issues at home, and the wider support they offer all play a part in young people's engagement and re-engagement with education. However, the young person's own determination to succeed in life is of crucial importance. Young people need to take advantage of all opportunities to develop their personal, intellectual and social skills, even when they are in challenging circumstances. Their persistence in striving to achieve their aspirations and ambitions will be critical to their re-engaging with education.

Endnote

Education has the potential to transform lives. The social inclusion of disengaged young people is a responsibility shared among all those involved with education and training, be it at an international, national, local or individual level. All too frequently young people at the extreme end of disengagement from education are pathologized with little regard to their individuality, their aspirations, their experiences and their potential. While it is hard to break intergenerational cycles of disadvantage, the differences of approach across countries, and the case study examples in this book, demonstrate that progress can be made and change achieved.

Too often those who are disengaged from education are pushed towards an education that is regarded as second best, towards low-level qualifications or vocational qualifications that have no status. They are often further marginalized by being placed in educational institutions that are also regarded as second best. While alternative educational providers, independent providers, FE institutions, and YOIs play a pivotal role in working with young people disengaged from education, it is incumbent on all of us to make a difference.

Chapter summary

- Education is fundamental to the ability of young people to prosper in a rapidly changing globalized society and economy.
- Disadvantage is transmitted across generations, although the extent to which this occurs varies between countries.
- Young people with little education and skills face increasing marginalization especially during times of economic recession. Those who disengage from education or drop out of education altogether are particularly vulnerable.
- The curricula offer and inflexible pathways in many developed countries contribute to disengagement.
- Young people can and do re-engage with education and training, but more needs to be done to optimize second-chance opportunities.
- Government, employers, schools, colleges, independent providers, YOIs, alternative educational providers, teacher education providers, families and young people all have an important role to play in preventing or dealing with student disengagement.

References

Abdelnoor, A. (2007) *Managed Moves*. London: Calouste Gulbenkian Foundation.

ACT Education and Training Directorate (2013) 'About Our Schools'. Online. www.det.act.gov.au/school_education?enrolling_in_an_act_public_school/ about_our_schools (accessed 11 February 2015).

Allen, T., Mehta, P., and Rutt, S. (2012) *Hidden Talents: A statistical overview of the participation patterns of young people aged 16–24*. Slough: NFER.

Alspaugh, J.W. (1998) 'Achievement loss associated with the transition to middle school and high school'. *Journal of Educational Research*, 92 (1), 20–5.

American Federation of Teachers (AFT) (2007) *Meeting the Challenge: Recruiting and retaining teachers in hard-to-staff schools*. Online. www.aft.org/sites/ default/files/hardtostaff_2007.pdf (accessed 8 March 2015).

Anderson, K., Brophy, M., McNeil, B., and Potter, D. (2010) *Opening the Door to Apprenticeships: Reaching young people who are disadvantaged and disengaged from apprenticeships. Paper 1: Setting the Scene*. London: The Young Foundation. Online. http://youngfoundation.org/wp-content/uploads/2012/10/ Opening-the-door-to-apprenticeships-February-2010.pdf (accessed 20 February 2015).

Anderson, L.W., Jacobs, J., Schramm, S., and Splittgerber, F. (2000) 'School transitions: Beginning of the end or a new beginning?' *International Journal of Education*, 33 (4), 325–39.

Appleton, J., Christenson, S., and Furlong, M. (2008). 'Student engagement with school: Critical conceptual and methodological issues of the construct'. *Psychology in the Schools*, 45 (5), 369–86.

Archer, L., Hollingworth, S., and Mendick, H. (2010) *Urban Youth and Schooling: The experiences and identities of educating 'at risk' young people*. Maidenhead: Open University Press.

Archive Incorporated (2006) *Identifying Potential Dropouts: Key lessons for building an early warning data system – A dual agenda of high standards and high graduation rates*. Online. www.achieve.org/files/FINAL-dropouts_0.pdf (accessed 2 September 2015).

Arico, F., and Lasselle, L. (2010) *Enhancing Interns' Aspirations towards the Labour Market through Skill-Acquisition: The second chance schools experience*. Online. https://crieff.files.wordpress.com/2012/08/dp1006.pdf (accessed 4 February 2015).

Arnold, C., Yeomans, J., Simpson, S., and Solomon, M. (2009) *Excluded from School: Complex discourses and psychological perspectives*. Stoke on Trent: Trentham Books.

Association of Colleges (AoC) (2015) *College Key Facts 2014–15*. Online. www. aoc.co.uk/sites/default/files/AOC%20KEY%20FACTS%202014.pdf (accessed 18 February 2015).

Attwood, G., and Croll, P. (2006) 'Truancy in secondary school pupils: Prevalence, trajectories and pupil perspectives'. *Research Papers in Education*, 21 (4), 467–84.

Attwood, G., Croll, P., and Hamilton, J. (2003) 'Re-engaging with education'. *Research Papers in Education*, 18 (1), 75–95.

Audit Commission (2010a) *Against the Odds: Re-engaging young people in education, employment or training*. London: Audit Commission.

— (2010b) *Against the Odds: Targeted briefing – young people with special educational needs*. London: Audit Commission.

Australian Curriculum, Assessment and Reporting Authority (ACARA) (2012) *Curriculum, Assessment and Reporting in Special Educational Needs and Disability: A thematic overview of recent literature*. Sydney: ACARA.

Australian Government (2009) *Compact with Young Australians: Increasing educational attainment of young people aged 15–24*. Canberra: Australian Government.

Australian Institute of Criminology (2011) 'Crime and Criminal Justice Statistics'. Online. www.aic.gov.au/statistics/criminaljustice/juveniles.html (accessed 27 January 2015).

Australian Research Alliance for Children and Youth (ARACY) (2013) *Inclusive Education for Students with Disability: A review of the best evidence in relation to theory and practice*. Canberra: Department of Education.

Bagley, C. (2013) '"Pass the Parcel". Are managed moves an effective intervention? Is there a role for Educational Psychologists in facilitating the process?' Ph.D. diss., Institute of Education, University of London.

Baird, J., Elwood, J., Duffy, G., Feiler, A., O'Boyle, A., Rose, J., and Stobart, G. (2011) *14–19 Centre Research Study: Educational reforms in schools and colleges in England. Annual report*. London: QCDA.

Baird, J., Rose, J., and McWhirter, A. (2012) 'So tell me what you want: A comparative study of FE college and other post-16 students' aspirations'. *Research in Post-Compulsory Education*, 17 (3), 293–310.

Balfanz, R., Herzog, L., and Mac Iver, D. (2007) 'Preventing student disengagement and keeping students on the graduation path in urban middle-grade schools: Early identification and effective interventions'. *Educational Psychologist*, 42 (4), 223–35.

Barber, M., and Mourshed, M. (2007) *How the World's Best Education Systems Come Out on Top*. London and New York: McKinsey Education.

Barnett, K. (2012) *Learner Case Management in VET and Other Tertiary Education: A literature review*. Adelaide: Australian Workplace Innovation and Social Research Centre, University of Adelaide. Online. www.adelaide. edu.au/wiser/pubs/DFEEST_CaseManagement_Publication.pdf (accessed 2 September 2015).

Baskin, T.W., Slaten, C.D., Crosby, N.R., Pufahl, T., Schneller, C.L., and Ladell, M. (2010) 'Efficacy of counseling and psychotherapy in schools: A meta-analytic review of treatment outcome studies'. *The Counseling Psychologist*, 38 (7), 878–903.

Bendigo Senior Secondary College (2014) 'Learning@NETschool'. Online. http:// www.bssc.edu.au/college/netschool/learning (accessed 26 August 2015).

Bielby, G., Judkins, M., O'Donnell, L., and McCrone, T. (2012) *Review of the Curriculum and Qualification Needs of Young People Who Are at Risk of Disengagement*. Slough: NFER.

Big Brothers Big Sisters (2014) 'Who we are'. Online. www.bbbsi.org/about-us/ (accessed 27 March 2015).

Big Picture Learning (2015) 'About Us'. Online. www.bigpicture.org/about-us/ (accessed 6 March 2015).

Birdwell, J., Grist, M., and Margo, J. (2011) *The Forgotten Half: A demos and private equity foundation report*. London: Demos.

Boggs, G. (2010) *Democracy's Colleges: The evolution of the community college in America*. American Association of Community Colleges. Online. www.aacc. nche.edu/AboutCC/whsummit/Documents/boggs_whsummitbrief.pdf (accessed 19 February 2015).

Bradley, H.L. (2009) *The Bradley Report: Lord Bradley's review of people with mental health problems or learning disabilities in the criminal justice system*. London: COI for the Department of Health. Online. www.rcpsych.ac.uk/pdf/ Bradleyreport.pdf (accessed 26 August 2015).

Bristow, M. (2013) 'An Exploration of the Use of PATH (a Person-Centred Planning Tool) by Educational Psychologists with Vulnerable and Challenging Pupils'. Ph.D. diss., Institute of Education, University of London.

Britton, J., Gregg, P., Macmillan, L., and Mitchell, S. (2011) *The Early Bird ... Preventing Young People from Becoming a NEET Statistic*. Bristol: Department of Economics and CMPO, University of Bristol.

Brown, B. (2013) 'The social treatment of ex-dropouts re-enrolled in secondary school in South Africa'. *Journal of Education and Learning*, 2 (4): 60–70.

Brown, J., and North, S. (2010) *Providing Support to Disadvantaged Learners in the Australian VET System: A report to the National VET Equity Advisory Council*. Camberwell, Victoria: Australian Council for Educational Research.

Bruce, M., Bridgeland, J.M., Fox, J.H., and Balfanz, R. (2011) *On Track for Success: The use of early warning indicator and intervention systems to build a grad nation*. Washington: Civic Enterprises.

Bryan, R., Treanor, M., and Hill, M. (2007) *Evaluation of Pilots to Improve Primary to Secondary School Transitions*. Edinburgh: Scottish Executive. Online. www.gov.scot/Resource/Doc/163851/0044590.pdf (accessed 26 August 2015).

Burgess, M., and Rodger, J. (2010) *14–19 Qualifications Strategy Research*. London: DfE. Online. www.gov.uk/government/uploads/system/uploads/ attachment_data/file/181765/DFE-RR055.pdf (accessed 2 September 2015).

Butler, H., Bond, L., Drew, S., Krelle, A., and Seal, I. (2005). *Doing it Differently: Improving young people's engagement with school*. Melbourne: Brotherhood of St Laurence.

Callanan, M., Kinsella, R., Graham, J., Turczuk, O., and Finch, S. (2009) *Pupils with Declining Attainment at Key Stages 3 and 4: Profiles, experiences and impacts of underachievement and disengagement*. London: DCSF.

Callanan, M., and Morrell, G. (2013) *Influences on Post-16 Participation: The views of 16- to 18-year olds studying part-time in further education (FE) colleges or not in employment, education or training (NEET)*. London: Institute for Fiscal Studies.

Canduela, J., Elliot, I., Lindsay, C., Macpherson, S., McQuaid, R.W., and Raeside, R. (2010) 'Partnerships to support early school leavers: School-college transitions and "winter leavers" in Scotland'. *Journal of Education and Work*, 23 (4), 339–62.

Carter, A. (2015) *Carter Review of Initial Teacher Training (ITT)*. London: DfE. Online. www.gov.uk/government/uploads/system/uploads/attachment_data/file/399957/Carter_Review.pdf (accessed 26 August 2015).

Carver, P.R., and Lewis, L. (2010) *Alternative Schools and Programs for Public School Students at Risk of Educational Failure: 2007–08*. Washington, DC: Government Printing Office. Online. http://nces.ed.gov/pubs2010/2010026.pdf (accessed 26 August 2015).

Casson, R., and Kingdon, G. (2007) *Tackling Low Educational Achievement*. York: Joseph Rowntree Foundation.

Cedefop (2010) *Guiding At-risk Youth Through Learning to Work: Lessons from across Europe*. Cedefop Research Paper No. 3. Luxembourg: Publications Office of the European Union. Online. www.cedefop.europa.eu/EN/Files/5503_en.pdf (accessed 14 February 2015).

Centre for Social Justice (CSJ) (2011) *No Excuses: A review of educational exclusion*. London: Centre for Social Justice.

Chapman, C., Laird, J., and KewalRamani, A. (2010) *Trends in High School Dropout and Completion Rates in the United States: 1972–2008. Compendium Report*. Washington, DC: National Center for Education Statistics, Institute of Education Sciences, US Department of Education.

Chevalier, A. (2004) *Parental Education and Child's Education. A natural experiment*. IZA Discussion Paper No. 1153. Bonn: IZA.

Choi, S., and Lemberger, M.E. (2010) 'Influence of a supervised mentoring program on the achievement of low-income South Korean students'. *Mentoring and Tutoring: Partnership in Learning*, 18 (3), 233–48.

Christenson, S.L., and Reschly, A.L. (2010) 'Check and connect: Enhancing school completion through student engagement'. In Doll, B., Pfohl, W., and Yoon, J. (eds), *Handbook of Youth Prevention Science*. New York: Routledge, 327–48.

Cities of Migration (2014) 'Second Chance School. Écoles de la deuxième chance'. Online. http://citiesofmigration.ca/good_idea/second-chance-school/ (accessed 2 February 2015).

Clark, T.C., Smith, J.M., Raphael, D., Jackson, C., Fleming, T., Denny, S., Ameratunga, S., and Robinson, E. (2010) *Youth'09: The health and wellbeing of young people in alternative education. A report on the needs of alternative education students in Auckland and Northland*. Auckland: University of Auckland.

Cole, S., O'Brien, J., Gadd, M., Ristucca, J., Wallace, D., and Gregory, M. (2005) *Helping Traumatized Children Learn: Supportive school environments for children traumatized by family violence*. Boston: Massachusetts Advocates for Children.

Coles, B., Godfrey, C., Keung, A., Parrott, S., and Bradshaw, J. (2010) *Estimating the Life-Time Cost of NEET: 16–18 year olds not in education, employment or training*. York: University of York.

Coles, B., Hutton, S., Bradshaw, J., Craig, G., Godfrey, C., and Johnson, J. (2002) *Literature Review of the Costs of Being 'Not in Education, Employment or Training' at Age 16–18*. Research Report RR347. Nottingham: DfES.

Cooper, M. (2013) *School-based Counselling in UK Secondary Schools: A review and critical evaluation*. Glasgow: University of Strathclyde.

Cooper, P., Kakos, M., and Jacobs, B. (2013) 'Best practice models and outcomes in the education of children with social, emotional and behavioural difficulties'. *Caise Review* 1, 2–24. Hong Kong: Faculty of Education, The University of Hong Kong. Online. http://tinyurl.com/oebr687 (accessed 11 February 2015).

Cowen, G., and Burgess, M. (2009) *Key Stage 4 Engagement Programme Evaluation*. London: DCSF.

Crawford, C., Duckworth, K., Vignoles A., and Wyness, G. (2011) *Young People's Education and Labour Market Choices Aged 16/17 to 18/19*. Research Report DFE-RR182. London: DfE.

Criminal Justice Inspection Northern Ireland (CJINI) (2011) *An Announced Inspection of Woodlands Juvenile Justice Centre*. Belfast: CJINI.

— (2013) *An Announced Inspection of Hydebank Wood Young Offenders Centre*. Belfast: CJINI.

Cushman, K., and Rogers, L. (2008) 'Middle school students talk about social forces in the classroom'. *Middle School Journal*, 39 (3), 14–24.

Cusworth, L., Bradshaw, J., Coles, B., Keung, A., and Chzhen, Y. (2009) *Understanding the Risks of Social Exclusion Across the Life Course: Youth and young adulthood*. London: Social Exclusion Task Force, Cabinet Office.

D'Addio, A.C. (2007) *Intergenerational Transmission of Disadvantage: Mobility or immobility across generations? A review of the evidence for OECD countries*. Paris: OECD.

Dale, R. (2010) *Early School Leaving: Lessons from research for policy makers*. An independent expert report submitted to the European Commission. Brussels: European Commission, DG Education and Culture. Online. www.nesse.fr/nesse/activities/reports/activities/reports/early-school-leaving-report (accessed 15 March 2015).

Daniels, H., Cole, T., Sellman, E., Sutton, J., and Visser, J. (2003) *Study of Young People Permanently Excluded from School*. Research Report RR405. London: DfES.

Davies, M., Lamb, S., and Doecke, E. (2011) *Strategic Review of Effective Re-Engagement Models for Disengaged Learners*. Australia: Victorian Department of Education and Early Childhood Development. Online. www.education.vic.gov.au/Documents/about/research/revreengage.pdf (accessed 2 September 2015).

Davis, L.M., Bozick, R., Steele, J.L., Saunders, J., and Miles, J.N.V. (2013) *Evaluating the Effectiveness of Correctional Education. A meta-analysis of programs that provide education to incarcerated adults*. Santa Monica, CA: RAND Corporation.

Demack, D., Drew, D., and Grimsley, M. (2000) 'Minding the gap: Ethnic, gender and social class differences in attainment at 16, 1988–97'. *Race Ethnicity and Education*, 3 (2), 117–43.

Department for Children, Schools and Families (DCSF) (2004) *Every Child Matters: Change for children in schools*. Nottingham: DCSF.

— (2009) *Raising the Participation Age: Supporting local areas to deliver*. Nottingham: DCSF.

— (2010) *Guidance on School Behaviour and Attendance Partnerships*. London: DCSF.

Department for Education (DfE) (2011) *Youth Cohort Study and Longitudinal Study of Young People in England: The activities and experiences of 19-year-olds: England 2010*. London: DfE.

— (2012a) *Statistical First Release. National Curriculum Assessments at Key Stage 2 in England, 2012 (Provisional)*. London: DfE.

— (2012b) *Teachers' Standards*. London: DfE.

— (2013) *Alternative Provision. Statutory guidance for local authorities*. London: DfE.

— (2014a) *Statistical First Release. Permanent and fixed period exclusions in England: 2012 to 2013*. London: DfE.

— (2014b) *Enrolment of 14 to 16-year-olds in Full-Time Further Education*. Online. www.gov.uk/government/publications/enrolment-of-14-to-16-year-olds-in-full-time-further-education (accessed 17th February 2015).

— (2014c) *Statistical Release. Children with special educational needs 2014: An analysis*. London: DfE.

— (2014d) *GCSE and Equivalent Results in England, 2012/13 (Revised)* (Statistical First Release 02/2013). London: DfE.

— (2014e) *Statistical first release. School workforce in England: November 2013*. London: DfE.

Department for Education and Employment (DfEE) (1999) *Social Inclusion: Pupil support* (Circular 10/99). London: DfEE.

Department for Education and Skills (DfES) (2002) *14–19: Opportunity and Excellence*. London: DfES.

— (2003) *21st Century Skills: Realising our potential*. London: DfES.

— (2005a) *Higher Standards for All*. London: HMSO.

— (2005b) *Supporting the New Agenda for Children's Services and Schools: The role of learning mentors and co-ordinators*. London: HMSO.

Department of Education and Early Childhood Development (DEECD) (2010) *Pathways to Re-engagement Through Flexible Learning Options: A policy direction for consultation*. Melbourne: DEECD.

Department of Justice, Canada (2013) *The Youth Criminal Justice Act: Summary and background*. Ottawa, ON: Department of Justice. Online. www.justice. gc.ca/eng/cj-jp/yj-jj/tools-outils/pdf/back-hist.pdf (accessed 28 March 2012).

Duffy, G., and Elwood, J. (2013) 'The perspectives of "disengaged" students in the 14–19 phase on motivations and barriers to learning within the contexts of institutions and classrooms'. *London Review of Education*, 11 (2), 112–26.

Dyer, F. (2014) *Supporting Young People Who Enter into Secure Care or Custody to Reintegrate into Communities* (Briefing Paper No. 04). Glasgow: Centre for Youth and Criminal Justice.

Eby, L.T., Allen, T.D., Evans, S.C., Ng, T., and Dubois, D. (2008) 'Does mentoring matter? A multidisciplinary meta-analysis comparing mentored and non-mentored individuals'. *Journal of Vocational Behaviour*, 72 (2), 254–67.

Education Review Office (ERO) (2013) *Provision for Students in Activity Centres*. New Zealand: ERO. Online. www.ero.govt.nz/National-Reports/Provision-for-Students-in-Activity-Centres-June-2013 (accessed 12 January 2015).

Elwick, A., Davis, M., Crehan, L., and Clay, B. (2013) *Improving Outcomes for Young Offenders: An international perspective*. Reading: CfBT Education Trust.

Eurofound (2012) *NEETs – Young People Not in Employment, Education or Training: Characteristics, costs and policy responses in Europe*. Luxembourg: Publications Office of the European Union.

— (2014) *Mapping Youth Transitions in Europe*. Luxembourg: Publications Office of the European Union.

European Commission (EC) (2001) *A New Impetus for European Youth*. COM (2001) 681. Online. https://cumulus.cedefop.europa.eu/files/vetelib/eu/leg/com/com_2001_0681_en.pdf (accessed 27 March 2015).

— (2010a) *Reducing Early School Leaving*. Brussels: EC.

— (2010b) *Youth on the Move*. Luxembourg: Publications Office of the European Union.

— (2010c) *Europe 2020: A European strategy for smart, sustainable and inclusive growth*. Online. http://ec.europa.eu/archives/commission_2010-2014/president/news/documents/pdf/20100303_1_en.pdf (accessed 30 March 2015).

— (2011) *Youth neither in Employment nor Education and Training (NEET)*. Presentation of data for the 27 member states, EMCO Contribution. Online. http://ec.europa.eu/social/BlobServlet?docId=6602&langId=en (accessed 2 September 2015).

— (2012) *Towards a Job-rich Recovery* (COM (2012) 173). Brussels: EC.

— (2014) *Annexes to the Communication from the Commission to the European Parliament, the Council, the European Economic and Social Committee and the Committee of the Regions. Taking stock of the Europe 2020 strategy for smart, sustainable and inclusive growth*. COM (2014) 130 final/2. Brussels: EC.

European Commission/EACEA/Eurydice/Cedefop (2014) *Tackling Early Leaving from Education and Training in Europe: Strategies, policies and measures*. Eurydice and Cedefop Report. Luxembourg: Publications Office of the European Union.

European Foundation for the Improvement of Living and Working Conditions (2012) *Recent Policy Developments Related to Those Not in Employment, Education and Training (NEETs)*. Dublin: Eurofound.

Evangelou, M., Taggart, B., Sylva, K., Melhuish, E., and Sammons, P. (2008) *What Makes a Successful Transition from Primary to Secondary School?* London: DCSF.

Evans, K., George, N., White, K., Sharp. C., Morris, M., Marshall, H., and Mehta, P. (2010) *Ensuring That All Children and Young People Make Sustained Progress and Remain Fully Engaged through All Transitions Between Key Stages* (C4EO Schools and Communities Research Review 2). London: Centre for Excellence and Outcomes in Children and Young People's Services.

Everson, H.T., and Millsap, R.E. (2005) *Everyone Gains: Extracurricular activities in high school and higher SAT scores*. College Board Research Report No. 2005–2. New York: College Entrance Examination Board.

Every Child a Chance Trust (2009a) *The Long Term Costs of Numeracy Difficulties*. London: Every Child a Chance Trust.

— (2009b) *The Long Term Costs of Literacy Difficulties*. London: Every Child a Chance Trust.

Ewen, M., and Topping, K. J. (2012) 'Personalised learning for young people with social, emotional and behavioural difficulties'. *Educational Psychology in Practice: Theory, research and practice in educational psychology*, 28 (3), 221–39.

Fabelo, T., Thompson, M., Plotkin, M., Carmichael, D., Marchbanks III, M., and Booth, E. (2011) *Breaking Schools' Rules: A statewide study of how school discipline relates to students' success and juvenile justice involvement.* New York: Council of State Governments Justice Center. Online. http://knowledgecenter.csg.org/drupal/system/files/Breaking_School_Rules.pdf (accessed 27 March 2015).

Farrington, D., and Welsh, B. (2003) 'Family-based prevention of offending: A meta-analysis'. *Australian and New Zealand Journal of Criminology*, 36 (2), 127–51.

— (2006) *Saving Children from a Life of Crime.* Oxford: Oxford University Press.

— (2007) *Saving Children from a Life of Crime: Early risk factors and effective intervention.* Oxford: Oxford University Press.

Filmer-Sankey, C., and McCrone, T. (2012) *Developing Indicators for Early Identification of Young People at Risk of Temporary Disconnection from Learning.* Slough: NFER.

Finn, J.D. (1989) 'Withdrawing from school'. *Review of Educational Research*, 59 (2), 117–42.

France, A., Sutton, L., Sandu, A., and Waring, A. (2007) *Making a Positive Contribution: The implications for youth work of Every Child Matters (Book 5).* Leicester: National Youth Agency.

Fredricks, J.A., Blumenfeld, P.C., and Paris, A. H. (2004) 'School engagement: Potential of the concept, state of the evidence'. *Review of Educational Research*, 74 (1), 59–109.

Fredricks, J.A., and Eccles, J. S. (2006) 'Is extracurricular participation associated with beneficial outcomes? Concurrent and longitudinal relations'. *Developmental Psychology*, 42 (4), 698–713.

Fredricks, J.A., Hackett, K., and Bregman, A. (2010) 'Participation in boys and girls clubs: motivation and stage environment fit'. *Journal of Community Psychology*, 38 (3), 369–85.

Frey, A., Ruchkin, V., Martin, A., and Schwab-Stone, M. (2009) 'Adolescents in transition: School and family characteristics in the development of violent behaviors entering high school'. *Child Psychiatry and Human Development*, 40 (1), 1–13.

Fullan, M., and Longworthy, M. (2014) *A Rich Seam: How new pedagogies find deep learning.* Harlow: Pearson.

Furlong, A. (2006) 'Not a very NEET solution: Representing problematic labour market transitions among early school-leavers'. *Work, Employment and Society*, 20 (3), 553–69.

Galton, M., Gray, J., and Ruddock, J. (1999) *The Impact of School Transitions and Transfers on Pupil Progress and Attainment.* London: HMSO.

— (2003) *Transfer and Transition in the Middle Years of Schooling (7–14): Continuities and discontinuities in learning.* London: DfES.

Gandara, P., and Contreras, F. (2009) *The Latino Education Crisis: The consequences of failed social policies.* Cambridge, MA: Harvard University Press.

GHK Consulting Ltd (2009) *Identifying Effective Practice in Raising Young People's Aspirations.* Coventry: Learning and Skills Council.

Gibbs, R., and Foskett, J. (2010) *Student Engagement in the Middle Years of Schooling (Years 7–10): A literature review*. New Zealand: Ministry of Education.

Glover, J., Webster, L., White, J., and Jones, N. (2012) *Developing the Secure Estate for Children and Young People in England and Wales: Young people's consultation report*. London: Youth Justice Board.

Golden, S., O'Donnell, L., and Rudd, P. (2005) *Evaluation of Increased Flexibility for 14 to 16 Year Olds Programme: The second year*. London: DfES.

Gopinathan, S., Tan, S., Yanping, F., Devi, L., Ramos, C., and Chao, E. (2008) *Transforming Teacher Education: Redefined professionals for 21st century schools*. Singapore: National Institute of Education.

Gracey, S., and Kelly, S. (2010) *Changing the NEET Mindset: Achieving more effective transitions between education and work*. London: Learning and Skills Network.

Gray, D.S., and Colucci-Gray, L. (2010) 'Challenges to ITE research in conditions of complexity'. *Journal of Education for Teaching: International research and pedagogy*, 36 (4), 425–39.

Grist, M., and Cheetham, P. (2011) *Experience Required: A Demos and V report on capability building and work-readiness*. London: Demos.

Grundiza, S., and Lopez Vilaplana, C. (2013) 'Intergenerational transmission of disadvantage statistics: Is the likelihood of poverty inherited?' Eurostat KS-SF-13-027-EN-N. Online. http://tinyurl.com/pwux7q9 (accessed 14 April 2015).

Guerin, B. (2014) *Breaking the Cycle of Disadvantage: Early childhood interventions and progression to higher education in Europe*. Cambridge and Brussels: RAND Europe.

Gutherson, P., Davies, H., and Daszkiewicz, T. (2011) *Achieving Successful Outcomes through Alternative Education Provision: An international literature review*. Reading: CfBT Education Trust.

Hallam, S. (2005) *Enhancing Motivation and Learning throughout the Lifespan* (Inaugural Professorial Lecture). London: Institute of Education.

— (2015) *The Power of Music*. London: International Music Education Research Centre.

Hallam, S., and Castle, F. (1999) *Evaluation of the Behaviour and Discipline Pilot Projects (1996–99)* Supported under the Standards Fund Programme. London: HMSO.

Hallam, S., Castle, F., and Rogers, L. with Creech, A., Rhamie, J., and Kokotsaki, D. (2005) *Research and Evaluation of the Behaviour Improvement Programme*. London: DfES.

Hallam, S., Mainwaring, D., and Rogers, L. (2012) 'Evaluation of SkillForce Zero Exclusions Pilot: Final report'. Online. http://eprints.ioe.ac.uk/16546/1/Final_report_SkillForce.pdf (accessed 5 September 2015).

Hallam, S., Mainwaring, D., Rogers, L., and Holmes, S. (2013) 'Evaluation of SkillForce Zero Exclusions Pilot: Perceptions of SkillForce and school staff and parents'. MS.

Hallam, S., and Rogers, L. (2008) *Improving Behaviour and Attendance at School*. Maidenhead: McGraw-Hill/Open University Press.

— (2010) 'Creativity'. In Hallam, S., and Creech, A. (eds) *Music Education in the 21st Century in the United Kingdom: Achievements, analysis and aspirations*. London: Institute of Education, 105–22.

Hallam, S., Rogers, L., Long, M., and Holmes, S. (2014a) *Evaluation of SkillForce Back on Track*. MS.

— (2014b) *Evaluation of SkillForce Ethos Pilot Primary Transition: Final report*. MS. London: Institute of Education.

Hallam, S., Rogers, L., and Rhamie, J. (2010) 'Staff perceptions of the success of an alternative curriculum: SkillForce'. *Emotional and Behavioural Difficulties*, 15 (1), 63–74.

Hallam, S., and Rogers, L. with Rhamie, J., Shaw, J., Rees, E., Haskins, H., Blackmore, J., and Hallam, J. (2003) *Evaluation of SkillForce*. London: Institute of Education.

Harkin, J. (2006) 'Treated like adults: 14–16 year-olds in Further Education'. *Research in Post-Compulsory Education*, 11 (3), 319–39.

Harper, H. (2013) *Outstanding Teaching in Lifelong Learning*. Maidenhead: McGraw-Hill/Open University Press.

Harper, A., Heron, M., Houghton E., O'Donnell S., and Sargent C. (2011) *International Evidence on Alternative Provision*. Slough: NFER.

Hartas, D. (2011) 'Young people's participation: Is disaffection another way of having a voice?' *Educational Psychology in Practice*, 27 (2), 103–15.

Hawley, J., Hall (Nevala), A-M., and Weber, T. (2012) *Effectiveness of Policy Measures to Increase the Employment Participation of Young People*. Ireland: Eurofound.

Haynes, G., McCrone, T., and Wade, P. (2013) 'Young people's decision making: The importance of high quality school-based careers education, information, advice and guidance'. *Research Papers in Education*, 28 (4), 459–82.

Hayward, N., Walker, S., O'Toole, G., Hewitson, C., Pugh, E., and Sundaram, P. (2009) *Engaging all Young People in Meaningful Learning after 16: A review*. London: Equality and Human Rights Commission.

Haywood, G., Wilde, S., and Williams, R. (2008) *Rathbone/Nuffield Review Engaging Youth Enquiry*. Online. http://tinyurl.com/oy539k3 (accessed 28 March 2015).

Hazel, N. (2008) *Cross-national Comparison of Youth Justice*. London: Youth Justice Board.

Hendriks, M., Luyten, H., Scheerens, J., Sleegers, P., and Steen, R. (2010) *Teachers' Professional Development: Europe in international comparison*. Luxembourg: Office for Official Publications of the European Union.

Her Majesty's Chief Inspector of Prisons (HMCIP) (2014a) *Report on an Unannounced Inspection of HMYOI Hindley*. London: HMIP.

— (2014b) *Report on an Unannounced Inspection of HMYOI Feltham (children and young people)*. London: HMIP.

Hilton, Z. (2006) 'Disaffection and school exclusion: Why are inclusion policies still not working in Scotland?' *Research Papers in Education*, 21 (3), 295–314.

Hines, M.T. (2007) 'Adolescent adjustment to the middle school transition: The intersection of divorce and gender in review'. *Research in Middle Level Education Online*, 31 (2), 1–15.

HM Government (2000) *The Young Offenders Institution Rules 2000*. Online. www.legislation.gov.uk/uksi/2000/3371/contents/made (accessed 27 February 2014).

— (2008) *The Education and Skills Act 2008*. Online. www.legislation.gov.uk/ukpga/2008/25/contents (accessed 6 August 2015).

— (2014) *An Evidence Review of the Drivers of Child Poverty for Families in Poverty Now and for Poor Children Growing Up to be Poor Adults*. London: HMSO.

HM Treasury and DfES (2007) *Policy Review of Children and Young People: A discussion paper*. London: HMSO.

Hockenberry, S. (2014) *Juveniles in Residential Placement, 2011* (Juvenile Offenders and Victims National Report Series Bulletin August 2014). Washington, DC: Office of Juvenile Justice and Delinquency Prevention. Online. http://ojjdp.gov/pubs/246826.pdf (accessed 28 March 2015).

Hodkinson, P., Beista, G., and James, D. (2007) 'Learning cultures and a cultural theory of learning'. In James, D., and Besta, G. (eds), *Improving Learning Cultures in Further Education*. London: Routledge, 21–37.

Hodson, P., Baddeley, A., Laycock, S., and Williams, S. (2005) 'Helping secondary schools to be more inclusive of Year 7 pupils with SEN'. *Educational Psychology in Practice*, 21 (1), 53–67.

Homel, J., Mavisakalyan, A., Nguyen, H.T., and Ryan, C. (2012) *School Completion: What we learn from different measures of family background. Longitudinal surveys of Australian youth*. Research Report No. 59. Adelaide: National Centre for Vocational Education and Research.

Hughes, D., and Gration, G. (2009) *Literature Review of Research on the Impact of Careers and Guidance-Related Interventions*. Reading: CfBT Education Trust.

Humphrey, N., and Lewis, S. (2008) 'What does "inclusion" mean for pupils on the autistic spectrum in mainstream secondary schools?' *Journal of Research in Special Education Needs,* 8 (3), 132–40.

Hurry, J., Brazier, L., and Wilson, A. (2010) *Improving the Literacy and Numeracy of Young People in Custody and in the Community*. London: National Research and Development Centre for Adult Literacy and Numeracy.

Hurry, J., Rogers, L., Simonot, M., and Wilson, A. (2012) *Inside Education: The aspirations and realities of prison education for under 25s in the London area. A report for Sir John Cass's Foundation*. Online. //www.ioe.ac.uk/Study_Departments/CECJS_John_Cass_Report.pdf (accessed 30 January 2015).

Hutchings, M., Maylor, U., Mendick, H., Menter, I., and Smart, S. (2006) *An Evaluation of Innovative Approaches to Teacher Training on the Teach First Programme: Final report to the Training and Development Agency for Schools*. London: Institute for Policy Studies in Education, London Metropolitan University.

Include Youth (2011) *Include Youth Submission to the Youth Justice Review Team's Review of the Youth Justice System in Northern Ireland*. Belfast: Include Youth.

Inspectorate Evaluation Studies (2010) *An Evaluation of Youthreach*. Dublin: Department for Education and Skills. Online. http://tinyurl.com/qyhcslo (accessed 31 January 2015).

Institute of Education (IOE) (University of London) and the National Foundation for Educational Research (NFER) (2014) *School Exclusion Trial Evaluation*. London: DfE.

Istance, D., Rees, G., and Williamson, H. (1994) *Young People Not in Education, Training or Employment in South Glamorgan*. Cardiff: South Glamorgan Training and Enterprise Council.

Jacobson, J., Bhardwa, B., Gyateng, T., Hunter, G., and Hough, M. (2010) *Punishing Disadvantage: A profile of children in custody*. London: Prison Reform Trust.

Johnson, J., Dyer, J., and Lockyer, B. (2013) *Perceptions of Learning Technologies by Marginalised Youth*. Stansted, Essex: Inclusion Trust.

Johnson, L. (2008) 'Relationship of instructional methods to student engagement in two public high schools'. *American Secondary Education*, 36 (2), 69–87.

Johnson, L., Smith, R., Willis, H., Levine, A., and Haywood, K. (2011) *The 2011 Horizon Report*. Austin, Texas: The New Media Consortium. Online. http://net.educause.edu/ir/library/pdf/HR2011.pdf (accessed 4 March 2015).

Keane, E., Aldridge, F.J., Costley, D., and Clark, T. (2012) 'Students with autism in regular classes: a long-term follow-up study of a satellite class transition model'. *International Journal of Inclusive Education*, 16 (10), 1001–17.

Keating, J., and Lamb, S. (2004) *Public Education and the Community: A report to the Education Foundation*. Melbourne: Education Foundation.

Kendall, S., Wilkin, A., Kinder, K., Gulliver, C., Harland, J., Martin, K., and White, R. (2007) *Effective Alternative Provision*. London: DCSF.

Kennedy, E. (2013) *Children and Young People in Custody 2012–13*. London: HMIP.

Kettlewell, K., Southcott, C., Stevens, E., and McCrone, T. (2012) *Engaging the Disengaged*. Slough: NFER.

KPMG (2009) *Re-engaging our Kids: A framework for educational provision to children and young people at risk of disengaging or disengaged from school*. Sydney: KPMG.

Lamb, S. (2011) 'TVET and the poor. Challenges and possibilities'. *International Journal of Training Research*, 9 (1–2), 60–71.

Landrum, T., Katsiyannis, A., and Archwamety, T. (2004) 'An analysis of placement and exit patterns of students with emotional or behavioral disorders'. *Behavioral Disorders*, 29 (2), 140–53.

Lawson, M.A., and Lawson, H.A. (2013) 'New conceptual frameworks for student engagement research policy and practice'. *Review of Educational Research*, 83 (3), 432–79.

Leach, L., Zepke, N., and Butler, P. (2014) 'Tertiary teachers' perspectives on their role in student engagement: A snapshot from Aotearoa New Zealand'. *Journal of Further and Higher Education*, 38 (1), 19–36.

Lloyd-Jones, S., Bowen, R., Holtom, D., Griffin, T., and Sims, J. (2010) *A Qualitative Research Study to Explore Young People's Disengagement from Learning*. Wales: Welsh Assembly Government Social Research.

Losen, D.J., and Gillespie, J. (2012) *Opportunities Suspended: The disparate impact of disciplinary exclusion from school*. Los Angeles: Civil Rights Project.

Lumby, J. (2011) 'Enjoyment and learning: Policy and secondary school learners' experience in England'. *British Educational Research Journal*, 37 (2), 247–64.

Lyche, C. (2010) *Taking on the completion challenge: A literature review on policies to prevent dropout and early school leaving* (OECD Education Working Papers No. 53). Online. http://dx.doi.org/10.1787/5km4m2t59cmr-en (accessed 10 February 2014).

Mac Iver, M.A., and Mac Iver, D.J. (2009) *Beyond the Indicators: An integrated school-level approach to dropout prevention.* Arlington, VA: Mid-Atlantic Equity Center, George Washington University Center for Equity and Excellence in Education.

MacBeath, J. (2011) 'Education of teachers: The English experience'. *Journal of Education for Teaching*, 37 (4), 377–86.

Machin, S., Marie, O., and Vujic, S. (2010) *The Crime Reducing Effect of Education* (CEP Discussion Paper No. 979). London: Centre for Economic Performance, London School of Economics.

Mackenzie, E., McMaugh, A., and O'Sullivan, K-A. (2012) 'Perceptions of primary to secondary school transitions: Challenge or threat?' *Issues in Educational Research*, 22 (3), 298–314.

Maguire, S., and Newton, B. with Fearn, H., Oakley, J., Williams, C., Miller, L., and Levesley, T. (2011) *Activity Agreement Pilots – Trialling Different Approaches to Re-engaging Young People Not in Education, Employment or Training (NEET): Evaluation of the 2009–10 extension.* London: DfE.

Mainwaring, D., and Hallam, S. (2010) '"Possible selves" of young people in a mainstream secondary school and a pupil referral unit: A comparison'. *Emotional and Behavioural Difficulties*, 15 (2), 153–69.

Malloy, J.M. (2013) 'The RENEW model: Supporting transition-age youth with emotional and behavioural challenges'. *Emotional and Behavioral Disorders in Youth*, Spring, 38–48.

Marson-Smith, H., Golden, S., and McCrone, T. (2009) *Widening 14–19 Choices: Support for young people making informed decisions.* Slough: NFER.

Martin, K., and White, R. (2012) *Alternative Provision for Young People with Special Educational Needs.* Slough: NFER.

Martin, K., Sharp, C., and Mehta, P. (2013) *Impact of the Summer Schools Programme on Pupils.* London: DfE.

Martinez, R.S., Aricak, O.T., Graves, M.N., Peters-Myszak, J., and Nellis, L. (2011) 'Changes in perceived social support and socioemotional adjustment across the elementary to junior high school transition'. *Journal of Youth Adolescence*, 40, (5), 519–30.

McCord, J., and Irwin, T. with Martynowicz, A. (2012) *Reviewing the Provision of Education for Young People in Detention: Rights, research and reflections on policy and practice.* CIP Special Report Series No. 3. Coleraine and Galway: Children and Youth Programme, UNESCO. Online. www.drugsandalcohol. ie/18120/1/CRRC_2012_REPORT_3.pdf (accessed 26 August 2015).

McCrone, T., and Filmer-Sankey, C. (2012) *A Review of Careers Professionals' Involvement with Schools in the UK.* Slough: NFER.

McGee, C., Ward, R., Gibbbons, J., and Harlow, A. (2003) *Transition to Secondary School: A literature review.* Wellington: Ministry of Education.

McGregor, G., and Mills, M. (2012) 'Alternative education sites and marginalised young people: "I wish there were more schools like this one"'. *International Journal of Inclusive Education*, 16 (8), 843–62.

McIntosh, S., and Houghton, N. (2005) *Disengagement from Secondary Education: A story retold*. London: Learning and Skills Network.

McNeil, B. (2008) *Working with Young Adults*. Leicester: NIACE.

McSherry, J. (2001) *Challenging Behaviour in Mainstream Schools: Practical strategies for effective intervention and reintegration*. London: David Fulton.

Measor, L., and Woods, P. (1984) *Changing Schools: Pupil perspectives on transfer to a comprehensive*. Milton Keynes: Open University Press.

Menzies, L. (2013) *Educational Aspirations: How English schools can work with parents to keep them on track*. York: Joseph Rowntree Foundation. Online. www.jrf.org.uk/sites/files/jrf/england-education-aspirations-summary.pdf (accessed 5 September 2015).

Mills, C., and Gale, T. (2009) *Schooling in Disadvantaged Communities: Playing the game from the back of the field*. London and New York: Springer Science and Business.

Mills, M., and McGregor, G. (2010) *Re-engaging Students in Education. Success factors in alternative schools*. Brisbane: Youth Affairs Network, Queensland.

Ministry of Business, Innovation and Employment (MBIE) (2013a) *Not in Employment, Education or Training: The long-term NEET spells of young people in New Zealand*. New Zealand: MBIE.

— (2013b) *Youth Labour Market Factsheet – March 2013*. New Zealand: MBIE. Online. www.dol.govt.nz/publications/lmr/pdfs/lmr-fs/lmr-fs-youth-mar13.pdf (accessed 4 February 2015).

Ministry of Education (2008) *A Study of Students' Transition from Primary to Secondary Schooling*. Wellington, New Zealand: Research Division.

Ministry of Education and Employment (MT) (2012) *Analysis of Feedback to the Consultation Process on the Draft National Curriculum Framework: Final Report*. Online. https://curriculum.gov.mt/en/Resources/The-NCF/Documents/Consult_Docs/Full%20Report.pdf (accessed 6 March 2015).

Ministry of Justice (MoJ) (2012) *Proven Re-offending Statistics Quarterly Bulletin April 2010 to March 2011: England and Wales*. London: MoJ.

— (2013) *Transforming Youth Custody: Putting education at the heart of detention*. Online. http://tinyurl.com/prwxdvy (accessed 25 January 2015).

— (2014) *Youth Justice Statistics 2012/13 England and Wales*. Online. www.gov.uk/government/uploads/system/uploads/attachment_data/file/278549/youth-justice-stats-2013.pdf (accessed 21 April 2014).

Mirza-Davies, J. (2014) *NEET: Young people Not in Education, Employment or Training* (House of Commons Library Standard Notes SN/EP/06705). London: House of Commons.

Mitchell, D. (2010) *Education That Fits: Review of international trends in the education of students with SEN: Final report*. Christchurch, New Zealand: College of Education, University of Canterbury. Online. www.educationcounts.govt.nz/__data/assets/pdf_file/0016/86011/Mitchell-Review-Final.pdf (accessed 11 February 2015).

Montalvo, G.P., Mansfield, E.A., and Miller, R.B. (2007) 'Liking or disliking the teacher: Student motivation, engagement and achievement'. *Evaluation and Research in Education*, 20 (3), 144–58.

Muncie, J. (2006) 'Repenalisation and rights: Explorations in comparative youth criminology'. *Howard Journal of Criminal Justice*, 45 (1), 42–70.

Murphy, P., McGuiness, A., and McDermott, T. (2010) *Review of Effective Practice in Juvenile Justice: Report for the Minister for Juvenile Justice.* Canberra: Noetic Solutions.

Murray, S., and Mitchell, J. (2015) 'Teaching practices that re-engage early school leavers in further education: An Australian study'. *Journal of Further and Higher Education.* DOI: 10.1080/0309877X.2014.971107.

National Audit Office (NAO) (2010) *The Youth Justice System in England and Wales: Reducing offending by young people.* London: NAO/MoJ.

— (2012) *Oversight of special education for young people aged 16–25.* London: NAO. Online. http://dera.ioe.ac.uk/13839/1/Oversight_9780215041906.pdf (accessed 2 September 2015).

National Institute of Adult and Continuing Education (NIACE) (2013) *Motivation and Barriers to Learning for Young People Not in Education, Employment or Training.* London: Department for Business, Innovation and Skills.

National Job Corp Association (NJCA) (2015) 'About Job Corp'. Online. http://njcaweb.org/about-job-corps/overview/ (accessed 26 August 2015).

Nechvoglod, L., and Beddie, F. (2010) *Hard to Reach Learners: What works in reaching and keeping them?* Melbourne, Victoria: Adult, Community and Further Education Board. Online. www.education.vic.gov.au/documents/about/research/hrl.doc (accessed 12 March 2015).

Nelson, J., and O'Donnell, L. (2012) *Approaches to Supporting Young People Not in Education, Employment or Training: A review.* Slough: NFER.

Nikolaraizi, M., and Hadjikakou, K. (2006) 'The role of educational experiences in the development of deaf identity'. *Journal of Deaf Studies and Deaf Education,* 11 (4), 477–92.

Norgate, R., Osborne, C., and Warhurst, A. (2013) 'Change in Myself-As-a-Learner Scale (MALS) scores as pupils transfer to and progress through secondary school'. *Educational Psychology in Practice: Theory, research and practice in educational psychology,* 29 (2), 122–37.

Norwich, B. (2008) 'What future for special schools and inclusion?' *British Journal of Special Education,* 35 (3), 136–43.

NSW Government (2012) *Educational Services Supporting Students with Disability.* Online. www.schools.nsw.edu.au/media/downloads/schoolsweb/studentsupport/programs/disabilitypgrms/eduservices-studisability.pdf (accessed 11 February 2015).

NSW Legislature Council (2010) *The Provision of Education to Students with a Disability or Special Needs.* Online. http://tinyurl.com/opdx5jr (accessed 27 August 2015).

Nuttall, C., and Woods, K. (2013) 'Effective intervention for school refusal behaviour'. *Educational Psychology in Practice: Theory, research and practice in educational psychology,* 29 (4), 347–66.

Obama, B. (2012) *State of the Union Address 2012.* Online. www.whitehouse.gov/the-press-office/2012/01/24/remarks-president-state-union-address (accessed 13 March 2015).

O'Donnell, L., Golden, S., McCrone, T., Rudd, P., and Walker, M. (2006) *Evaluation of Increased Flexibility for 14–16 Year-Olds Programme: Delivery for cohorts 3 and 4 and the future.* London: DfES.

OECD (2005) *Teachers Matter: Attracting, developing and retaining effective teachers*. Paris: OECD.

— (2008a) *Jobs for Youth: Japan*. Paris: OECD.

— (2008b) *Jobs for Youth: Korea*. Paris: OECD.

— (2011) *Strong Performers and Successful Reformers in Education: Lessons from PISA for the United States*. Paris: OECD.

— (2012a) *Equity and Quality in Education: Supporting disadvantaged students and schools*. Paris: OECD Publishing.

— (2012b) *Special Educational Needs (SEN) OECD Child well-being Module CX3.1*. OECD Social Policy Division – Directorate or Employment, Labour and Social Affairs. Online. www.oecd.org/els/family/50325299.pdf (accessed 28 March 2015).

— (2013a) *Education at a Glance 2013: OECD Indicators*. Paris: OECD Publishing.

— (2013b) *The OECD Action Plan for Youth: Giving youth a better start in the labour market*. Paris: OECD Publishing.

— (2014a) *Education at a Glance 2014: OECD indicators*. Paris: OECD Publishing.

— (2014b) *Pisa in Focus. Who are the school truants?* Paris: OCED Publishing. Online. www.oecd.org/pisa/pisaproducts/pisainfocus/PISA-in-Focus-n35-(eng)-FINAL.pdf (accessed 27 March 2015).

— (2014c) *G20-OECD-EC Conference on Quality Apprenticeships for Giving Youth a Better Start in the Labour Market: Background paper prepared by the OECD*. Paris: OECD Publishing.

— (2014d) *Skills beyond schools: Synthesis report, OECD reviews of vocational education and training*. Paris: OECD Publishing.

Office of the Children's Commissioner (OCC) (2012) '*They Never Give Up on You': Office of the Children's Commissioner's School Exclusions Inquiry*. London: OCC.

Ofsted (2002) *Changing Schools: An evaluation of the effectiveness of transfer arrangements at age 11*. London: Ofsted.

— (2006) *Evaluation of the Impact of Learning Support Units*. London: Ofsted.

— (2008) *Good Practice in Re-engaging Disaffected and Reluctant Students in Secondary Schools*. London: Ofsted.

— (2009) *Identifying Good Practice: A survey of college provision in arts and media*. London: Ofsted.

— (2010a) *Reducing the Numbers of Young People Not in Education, Employment or Training: What works and why*. London: Ofsted.

— (2010b) *Transition through Detention and Custody: Arrangements for learning and skills for young people in custodial or secure settings*. London: Ofsted.

— (2010c) *The Special Educational Needs and Disability Review*. London: Ofsted.

— (2010d) *Children Missing from Education: The actions taken to prevent children from missing education or becoming 'lost to the system'*. London: Ofsted.

— (2011a) *Progression Post-16 for Learners with Learning Difficulties and/or Disabilities*. London: Ofsted.

— (2011b) *Alternative Provision*. London: Ofsted.

— (2012) *Apprenticeships for Young People: A good practice report.* London: Ofsted.

— (2013) *Going in the Right Direction? Careers guidance in schools from September 2012.* London: Ofsted.

— (2014a) *Teaching, Learning and Assessment in Further Education and Skills – What works and why.* London: Ofsted.

— (2014b) *Supporting Young People to Participate in Education and Training.* London: Ofsted.

— (2014c) *Alternative Provision. A Report on the Findings From the First Year of a Three-year Survey.* London: Ofsted.

Ontario Ministry of Education (2010) *Supervised Alternative Learning: Policy and implementation.* Toronto: Ministry of Education. Online. www.edu.gov.on.ca/eng/policyfunding/SAL2011English.pdf (accessed 12 January 2015).

— (2011) 'The Student Success Strategy'. Online. www.edu.gov.on.ca/eng/teachers/studentsuccess/strategy.html (accessed 15 January 2015).

Oreopoulos, P., Page, M.E., and Stevens A.H. (2003) *Does Human Capital Transfer from Parent to Child? The intergenerational effects of compulsory schooling* (NBER Working Paper No. 10164). Cambridge, MA: National Bureau of Economic Research.

Osler, A., Watling, R., and Busher, H. (2001) *Reasons for Exclusion from School.* London: DfEE.

Panayiotopoulos, C., and Kerfoot, M. (2007) 'Early intervention and prevention for children excluded from primary schools'. *International Journal of Inclusive Education*, 11 (1), 59–80.

Parsons, C., and Howlett, K. (2000) *Investigating the Reintegration of Permanently Excluded Young People in England.* Ely: Include.

Passey, D. (2012) *Independent Evaluation of the Little Big Planet 2 Project in Wolverhampton's Local Education Partnership Schools: Outcomes and impacts.* Lancaster: Department of Educational Research, Lancaster University. Online. http://eprints.lancs.ac.uk/59658/1/LBP2_evaluation_report_final.pdf (accessed 3 March 2015).

Passey, D., and Davies, P. (2010) *Technology to Support Young People 16 to 18 Years of Age who are Not in Employment, Education or Training (NEET): A local authority landscape review. Final report.* Lancaster: Department of Educational Research, Lancaster University.

Patrick, H., Ryan, A., and Kaplan, A. (2007) 'Early adolescents' perceptions of the classroom social environments, motivational beliefs, and engagement'. *Journal of Educational Psychology*, 99 (1), 83–98.

Pellegrini, D.W. (2007) 'School non-attendance: Definitions, meanings, responses, interventions'. *Educational Psychology in Practice: Theory, research and practice in educational psychology,* 23 (1), 63–77.

Porche, M.V., Fortuna, L.R., Lin, J., and Alegria, M. (2011) 'Childhood trauma and psychiatric disorders as correlates of school dropout in a national sample of young adults'. *Child Development*, 82 (3), 982–98.

Portland State University (2015) 'Teacher Pathways Program'. Online. www.pdx.edu/education/pathways (accessed 8 March 2015).

Power, C. (2007) 'Educational research, policy and practice in an era of globalisation'. *Educational Research for Policy and Practice,* 6 (2), 87–100.

Prince's Trust (2015a) 'How to Start a Business: The Enterprise Programme'. Online. www.princes-trust.org.uk/need_help/enterprise_programme.aspx (accessed 19 February 2015).

— (2015b) 'Get Started'. Online. www.princes-trust.org.uk/need_help/courses/ get_started.aspx (accessed 29 March 2015).

Prison Reform Trust (2014) *Bromley Briefings Prison Factfile. Autumn 2014.* Online.http://tinyurl.com/oek2k3e (accessed 26 August 2015).

QA Research (2012) *Young People Not in Education, Employment or Training (NEET) and Music Making.* London: Youth Music.

Qualifications and Curriculum Authority (QCA) (2004) *Designing a Personalised Curriculum for Alternative Provision at Key Stage 4.* London: QCA.

Rhodes, J.E., and DuBois, D.L. (2006) 'Understanding and facilitating the youth mentoring movement'. *Social Policy Report*, 20 (3), 3–19.

Rice, F., Frederickson, N., and Seymour, J. (2010) 'Assessing pupil concerns about transition to secondary school'. *British Journal of Educational Psychology*, 81 (2), 244–63.

Richmond, E. (2013) 'High School Graduation Rate Hits 40-Year Peak in the US'. Online. www.theatlantic.com/national/archive/2013/06/high-school-graduation-rate-hits-40-year-peak-in-the-us/276604/ (accessed 12 March 2015).

Roberts, A., and Wignall, L. (2010) *Briefing on Foundation Skills for the National VET Equity Advisory Council.* Online. http://cgea-pd.wikispaces.com/file/view/ Briefing+on+Foundation+Skills_Anita+Roberts+%26+Louise+Wignall.pdf (accessed 19 February 2015).

Robinson, L., Lamb, S., and Walstab, A. (2010) *How Young People are Faring 2010.* Melbourne: The Foundation for Young Australians.

Rogers, L., Hurry, J., Simonot, M., and Wilson, A. (2014a) 'The aspirations and realities of prison education for under-25s in the London area'. *London Review of Education*, 12 (2), 184–96.

Rogers, L., Simonot, M., and Nartey, A. (2014b) *Prison Educators: Professionalism against the odds.* London: UCU.

Ross, A. (2009) *Disengagement from Education among 14–16-Year-Olds.* London: DCSF.

Rovner, J. (2014) *Slow to Act: State responses to 2012 Supreme Court mandate on life without parole.* Washington: The Sentencing Project.

Rudd, P., and Walker, M. (2010) *Children and Young People's Views on Web 2.0 Technologies* (LGA Research Report). Slough: NFER.

Rumberger, R.W. (2011) *Dropping Out: Why students drop out of high school and what can be done about it.* Cambridge, MA: Harvard University Press.

Rumberger, R.W., and Lim, S. (2009) *Why Students Drop Out of School: A review of 25 years of research.* California Dropout Research Project Policy Brief No. 15. Santa Barbara, CA: UCSB.

Rumberger, R.W., and Thomas, S.L. (2000) 'The distribution of dropout and turnover rates among urban and suburban high schools'. *Sociology of Education*, 73 (1), 39–67.

Rupani, P., Haughey, N., and Cooper, M. (2012) 'The impact of school-based counselling on young people's capacity to study and learn'. *British Journal of Guidance and Counselling*, 40 (5), 499–514.

Russell, L., and Thomson, P. (2011) 'Girls and gender in alternative education provision'. *Ethnography and Education*, 6 (3), 293–308.

Sacher, M. (2006) *Survey Aims to Help at Risk Children.* Sydney: University of Sydney.

Sahlberg, P., and Boce, E. (2010) 'Are teachers teaching for a knowledge society?' *Teachers and Teaching,* 16 (1), 31–48.

Sahlberg, P., Broadfoot, P., Coolahan, J., Furlong, J., and Kirk, G. (2014) *Aspiring to Excellence: Final report of the international review panel on the structure of initial teacher education in Northern Ireland.* Online. www.delni.gov.uk/aspiring-to-excellence-review-panel-final-report.pdf (accessed 6 March 2015).

Schoof, U. (2006) *Stimulating Youth Entrepreneurship: Barriers and incentives to enterprise start-ups by young people* (SEED working paper No 76). Geneva: International Labour Office. Online. www.ilo.org/youthmakingithappen/PDF/WP76-2006-Rev.pdf (accessed 19 February 2015).

Schuller, T. (2009) *Crime and Lifelong Learning.* Leicester: NIACE.

Scottish Government (2010) *Making an Impact: Community and learning development case studies.* Edinburgh: Scottish Government.

— (2012) *Statistical Bulletin Crime and Justice Series: Prison statistics and population projections Scotland: 2011–12.* Scotland: Scottish Government.

Serafino, P., and Tonkin, R. (2014) *Intergenerational Transmission of Disadvantage in the UK and EU.* London: Office for National Statistics

Sink, C.A., Akos, P., Turnbull, R.J., and Mvududu, N. (2008) 'An investigation of comprehensive school counseling programs and academic achievement in Washington state middle schools'. *Professional School Counseling*, 12 (1), 43–53.

Simm, C., Page, R., and Miller, L. (2007) *Reasons for Early Leaving from FE and Work-Based Learning Courses.* London: DfES.

Simmons, R., and Thompson, R. (2011) 'Education and training for young people at risk of becoming NEET: Findings from an ethnographic study of work-based learning programmes'. *Educational Studies,* 37 (4), 447–50.

Skills Australia (2010) *Creating a Future Direction for Australian Vocation Education and Training: A discussion paper on the future of the VET system.* Skills Australia. Online. http://tinyurl.com/pslamta (accessed 27 August 2015).

Skinner, E.A., Furrer, C., Marchand, G., and Kindermann, T. (2008) 'Engagement and disaffection in the classroom: Part of a larger motivational dynamic?' *Journal of Educational Psychology,* 100 (4), 765–81.

Smith, J.S., Akos, P., Lim, S., and Wiley, S. (2008) 'Student and stakeholder perceptions of the transition to high school'. *High School Journal*, 91 (3), 32–42.

Snyder, T.D., and Dillow, S.A. (2012) *Digest of Education Statistics 2011.* NCES 2012-001. Washington, DC: National Center for Education Statistics, Institute of Education Sciences, UK Department of Education. Online. http://nces.ed.gov/pubs2012/2012001.pdf (accessed 9 February 2015).

Social Exclusion Task Force (2008) *Think Family: Improving the life chances of families at risk.* London: Cabinet Office.

Social Exclusion Unit (SEU) (1999) *Bridging the Gap: New opportunities for 16–18-year-olds not in education, employment or training.* London: Stationery Office.

— (2002) *Reducing Re-offending by Ex-prisoners: Report by the Social Exclusion Unit*. London: Office of the Deputy Prime Minister.

Sodha, S. and Guglielmi, S. (2009) *A Stitch in Time: Tackling educational disengagement. Interim report*. London: Demos.

Spielhofer, T., Benton, T., Evans, K., Featherstone, G., Golden, S., Nelson, L., and Smith, P. (2009) *Increasing Participation: Understanding young people who do not participate in education or training at 16 or 17*. Slough: NFER.

Steedman, H. (2010) *The State of Apprenticeship in 2010: International comparisons: Australia, Austria, England, France, Germany, Ireland, Sweden, Switzerland*. A Report for the Apprenticeship Ambassadors Network. London: LSE.

Steedman, H., and Stoney, S. (2004) *Disengagement 14–16: Context and evidence*. CEP Discussion paper No. 654. Online. http://cep.lse.ac.uk/pubs/download/dp0654.pdf (accessed 27 August 2015).

Steer, A. (2009) *Review of Pupil Behaviour Interim Report 4*. London: Institute of Education.

Stevenson, B., Watt, G., Clark, I., Simpson, L., and Stuart, A. (2011) *Evaluation of the Activity Agreements Pilots*. Edinburgh: Scottish Government Research Centre.

Stillwell, R. (2010) *Public School Graduates and Dropouts from the Common Core of Data: School year 2007–08* (NCES No. 341). Washington, DC: National Center for Education Statistics. Online. http://nces.ed.gov/pubs2010/2010341.pdf (accessed 12 March 2015).

Strahan, D. (2008) 'Successful teachers develop academic momentum with reluctant students'. *Middle School Journal*, 39 (5), 4–12.

Strand, S., and Winston, J. (2008) 'Educational aspirations in inner city schools'. *Educational Studies*, 34 (4), 249–67.

Sullivan, A.M., Johnson, B., Owens, L., and Conway, R. (2014) 'Punish them or engage them? Teachers' views of unproductive student behaviours in the classroom'. *Australian Journal of Teacher Education*, 39 (6), 43–56.

Sutton Trust (2011) *Improving the Impact of Teachers on Pupil Achievement in the UK – Interim Findings*. London: Sutton Trust.

Sweet, R., Volkoff, V., Watts, A.G., Keating, K., Helme, S., Rice, S., and Pannel, S. (2010) *Making Career Development Core Business*. Melbourne: Office for Policy, Research and Innovation Department of Education and Early Childhood Development and Department of Business and Innovation.

Swift, J., and Fisher, R. (2012) 'Choosing vocational education: Some views from young people in West Yorkshire'. *Research in Post-Compulsory Education*, 17 (2), 207–21.

Szira, J., and Nemeth, S. (2007) *Advancing Education of Roma in Hungary: Country assessment and the Roma Education Fund's strategic directions*. Budapest: Roma Education Fund.

Talbot, J. (2010) *Seen and Heard: Supporting vulnerable children in the youth justice system*. London: Prison Reform Trust.

Tanner, E., Purdon, S., D'Souza, J., and Finch, S. (2009) *Activity Agreement Pilots Quantitative Evaluation*. London: DCSF.

Taylor, C. (2012a) *Improving Attendance at School*. London: DfE.

— (2012b) *Improving Alternative Provision*. London: DfE.

te Riele, K. (2014) *Putting the Jigsaw Together: Flexible learning programs in Australia. Final Report*. Melbourne: The Victoria Institute for Education, Diversity and Lifelong Learning.

Thambirajah, M.S., Grandison, K.J., and De-Hayes, L. (2008) *Understanding School Refusal: A handbook for professionals in education, health and social care*. London and Philadelphia: Jessica Kingsley.

Thapa, A., Cohen, J., Guffey, S., and Higgins-D'Alessandro, A. (2013) 'A review of school climate research'. *Review of Educational Research*, 83 (3), 357–85.

Thomas, S., and Hillman, K. (2010) *Against the Odds: Influences on the post-school success of low performers*. Adelaide: National Centre for Vocational Education Research.

Thomson, P., and Pennacchia, J. (2014) *What's the Alternative? Effective support for young people disengaging from education*. London: The Prince's Trust.

Traag T., and van der Velden, R.K.W. (2011) 'Early school-leaving in the Netherlands: The role of family resources, school composition and background characteristics in early school-leaving in lower secondary education'. *Irish Educational Studies*, 30 (1), 45–62.

Tye, D. (2009) *HM Inspectorate of Prisons, Youth Justice Board: Children and young people in custody 2008–2009: An analysis of the experiences of 15–18-year-olds in prison*. London: HMIP.

UNESCO (1994) *World Conference on Special Needs Education: Access and quality*. Salamanca, Spain: Ministry of Education and Science, Madrid: UNESCO.

— (2009) *Policy Guidelines on Inclusion in Education*. France: UNESCO.

UNICEF (2014) *UNICEF Statistics Secondary Education: Current status and progress*. Online. http://data.unicef.org/education/secondary#current_status (accessed 26 March 2015).

United Nations (1989) *Convention on the Rights of the Child*. Resolution No. 44/25. Online. www.ohchr.org/Documents/ProfessionalInterest/crc.pdf (accessed 2 September 2015).

— (1990) *Rules for the Protection of Juveniles Deprived of their Liberty ('The Havana Rules')* (Resolution No. 45/113).

United Nations Committee on the Rights of the Child (2007) *General Comment No. 10 (2007): Children's rights in juvenile justice (CRC/C/CG/10)*. Geneva: Office of the United Nations High Commissioner for Human Rights. Online. http://www2.ohchr.org/english/bodies/crc/docs/CRC.C.GC.10.pdf (accessed 2 September 2015).

US Department of Education (2012) *The Transformed Civil Rights Data Collection: Revealing new truths about our nation's schools*. Washington, DC: Office of Civil Rights.

Vermont Secondary College (2014) *Year 7 Transition Program*. Online. www.vermontsc.vic.edu.au/yr7_transition (accessed 10 March 2015).

Victoria Institute for Education, Diversity and Lifelong Learning (2014) 'The Pavilion School'. Melbourne: Victoria University. Online. http://dusseldorp.org.au/priorities/alternative-learning/case-studies/pavilion-school/ (accessed 6 March 2015).

Villegas, A.M., and Davis, D. (2007) 'Approaches to diversifying the teaching force. Attending to issues of recruitment, preparation, and retention'. *Teacher Education Quarterly*, 34 (4), 137–47.

Visher, M.G., Altuna, J.N., and Safran, S. (2013) *Making it Happen: How career academies can build college and career exploration programs*. New York: MDRC.

Walden, G., and Troltsch, K. (2011) 'Apprenticeship training in Germany: Still a future-oriented model for recruiting skilled workers?' *Journal of Vocational Education and Training*, 63 (3), 305–22.

Walker, J., and Donaldson, C. (2011) *Intervening to Improve Outcomes for Vulnerable Young People: A review of the evidence*. London: DfE.

Walsh, L., Lemon, B., Black, R., Mangan, C., and Collin, P. (2011) *The Role of Technology in Engaging Disengaged Youth: Final report*. Canberra: Australian Flexible Learning Framework.

Ward, R. (2000) 'Transfer from middle to secondary school: A New Zealand study'. *International Journal of Educational Research*, 33 (4), 365–74.

West, P., Sweeting, H., and Young, R. (2010) 'Transition matters: Pupils' experiences of the primary–secondary school transition in the West of Scotland and consequences for well-being and attainment'. *Research Papers in Education*, 25 (1), 21–50.

Wheeler, M.E., Keller, T.E., and DuBois, D.L. (2010) 'Review of three recent randomized trials of school-based mentoring: Making sense of mixed findings'. *Social Policy Report*, 24 (3), 3–27.

White, R., Martin, K., and Jeffes, J. (2012*) The Back on Track Alternative Provision Pilots Final Report*. London: DfE.

Wilkin, A., Derrington, C., White, R., Martin, K., Foster, B., Kinder, K., Rutt, S. (2009) *Improving the Outcomes for Gypsy, Roma and Traveller Pupils: Literature review*. London: DCSF.

Wilkins, J., and Huckabee, S. (2014) *A Literature Map of Dropout Prevention Interventions for Students with Disabilities*. Clemson, SC: National Dropout Prevention Center for Students with Disabilities, Clemson University.

Wilson, A. (2010) 'Interrupted life: The criminal justice system as a disruptive force in the lives of young offenders'. *Prison Service Journal*, 189, 3–8.

Wolf, A. (2011) *Review of Vocational Education: The Wolf report*. London: DfE and DBIS.

Woodin, T., McCulloch, G., and Cowan, S. (2013) *Secondary Education and the Raising of the School-Leaving Age: Coming of age?* Basingstoke: Palgrave Macmillan.

Wylie, C., and Hipkins, R. (2006) *Growing Independence: Competent learners at 14*. Wellington: New Zealand Council for Educational Research.

Yates, S., and Payne, M. (2006) 'Not so NEET'? A critique of the use of "NEET" in setting targets for interventions with young people'. *Journal of Youth Studies*, 9 (3), 329–44.

YouthBuild US (2014) *YouthBuild Program Directory*. Online. www.youthbuild. org/program-directory (accessed 31 January 2015).

Zepke, N., and Leach, L. (2010) 'Improving Student Engagement: Ten proposals for action'. *Active Learning in Higher Education*, 11 (3), 167–77.

Index